GOD, ROD STEWART & ME

Rocking with Rod Stewart, Enlightenment, Mayhem in Morocco, Riots in Harlem, World Revolution, Meeting God, Madness and Working for the Council

By

Steve Attridge

More an exhumation than an autobiography and a book for anyone who has ever been young and reckless

A Wild Wolf Publication

Published by Wild Wolf Publishing in 2023

First print

ISBN: 9798396933309
Also available in E-Book edition

www.wildwolfpublishing.com

For over a century, the Oxford English Dictionary has defined Enlightenment as "shallow and pretentious intellectualism, unreasonable contempt for tradition and authority." This appears to the author to be a fair and accurate description of this book.

Enlightenment: To relieve a person of a superstition or prejudice. **Oxford Dictionary**

Enlightenment: to relieve a person of something, such as a wallet, an idea, girlfriend, or sanity. **The Dictionary of Enlightenment and Revolution** (as yet unwritten) By Steve Attridge

This book is dedicated to everyone mentioned in it, living and dead or otherwise occupied

CONTENTS PAGE

Introduction of Sorts

You made a first class fool out of me
But I'm as blind as a fool can be…

It wasn't just Maggie May that made a fool out of me but the whole universe as I tumbled in the dark of an Epping Forest night down a twenty foot ditch, so relaxed on a brain frying cocktail of white wine and brown bombers that I didn't break my neck, as Rod Stewart and the Faces finished their set and had a few more port and brandies in the dressing room. It had been a great night. Little did I know that within a few months I would be trailblazing across the United States with the Faces, Free and John Baldry, from Miami to Madison Square Gardens, leaving most of my wits still blowing in the mid-west breezes, finally landing in a hallucinatory heap in Times Square and starting a riot in Harlem that would see me catapulted from the USA to a madhouse in Kent. What more could a young boy hope for?

It was the early 1970s and for several years prior pop stars had been going down like flies on a blowlamp. Mama Cass was fatally assaulted in bed by a cheese sandwich, Jimi Hendrix was murdered by his own vomit, Brian Jones was drowned by a bald jealous builder named Frank, Jim Morrison mortally wounded by a hot bath in Paris and his heart said 'Enough. Enough. Je suis mort", Janis Joplin fell into a vat of Southern Comfort, and my friend Martin Jegan suffered a fatal brain hemorrhage after we listened to *Strawberry Fields Forever.* Let the good times roll. Jesus Christ, who next? I wondered. I was well acquainted with the Grim Reaper. The bastard had already taken a host of rabbits, hamsters, guinea pigs, a dog, lizards, newts, tropical fish, goldfish, terrapins, my grandparents and hundreds of ladybirds who never got the hang of living in matchboxes. In a few short years my fated star crossed with those of Brian Jones, Tiny Tim, Hendrix, Free, John Baldry and the Faces. But it was working in the Council Parks that was to give me a useful life lesson in death and insanity.

A PROLOGUE OF SORTS – Brian Jones, The Rolling Stone that started it

As he sat across from me sipping his bitter and chain smoking I felt that *Sympathy for the Devil* was almost as good as Psalm 23. *Pleased to meet you. Hope you guessed my name. The Lord is my shepherd; I shall not want. He maketh me to lie down in green pastures: he leadeth me beside the still waters. I rode a tank held a general's rank when the blitzkrieg raged and the bodies stank. He restoreth my soul: he leadeth me in the paths of righteousness for his name's sake. Just as every cop is a criminal and all the sinners saints, as heads is tails just call me Lucifer 'Cos I'm in need of some restraint.* I was only sixteen but I knew from then on I'd be caught in the headlight glare of solid gold opposites. Contradictions would be my Light and my Armageddon. The sun and the moon beckoned simultaneously. Brian Jones' music would be one of its soundtracks, even as I fell and frolicked in the laddish booze and drug fuelled bonhomie of Rod Stewart and the Faces.

Brian Jones was the Prince of Darkness and Little Boy Lost blues junkie, the bright blonde harpy the Rolling Stones could never erase. His ghost still shimmers in their ludicrous dollar-strewn Cadillac voyage to old age. He is the bright spot Keith and Mick have tried for over forty years to rub out, and failed. His appetites for sex, drugs and self-destruction were the unholy trinity determined to destroy him. A doomed mischief-hunting pixie who could pick up any instrument and make it sing. The driving sitar on *Paint it Black*, the dirty slide guitar on *I Wanna Be Your Man,* mellotron on *2000 Light Years From Home*, tambura on *Mother's Little Helper.* The list is long. I was entranced by him. He'd been down to the Crossroads and came back with a sack full of music and a hunger for annihilation.

I was a child when I first met him in 1964 and the Rolling Stones embarked on a six week tour, bottom of the bill and John "Wild Wind" Leyton top. By the end of the tour the Stones were top of the bill. Their noisy rag taggle dishabille cocktail of blues, rock and shock, gave a generation something to scream about. I spent my newspaper round and pools delivery job money on a ticket and programme. I waited outside the Edmonton Granada as the performers arrived. I asked Brian Jones how many cigarettes he smoked a day and he smiled and said 'A hundred.' I was hooked. This was a god worth fighting for. No one could hear them play for the screaming but I was entranced by Bill Wyman's solid presence and unique bass stance, Keith Richards jumping like a demented monkey, Jagger mincing and strutting his stuff, but mostly by Brian Jones playing his Vox teardrop guitar in a private universe of Cool. I got caned the next day at school for showing the programme to my mates and was told by Basher Briggs, the PE Teacher, that he didn't like little boys growing up too soon. My stinging bum cheeks bore testimony to another nail in the baroque coffin of unfathomable and paranoid conventionality.

Jump five years and Brian Jones was sacked by the Stones for being a dysfunctional degenerate with a string of illiterate children, a drug abuse problem that could halt a locomotive, and a reputation for being a prize dick. All heroic plus factors for which he should be commended in my Book of Life, but the Stones had other ideas. I hitchhiked down to Pooh Corner, Cotchford Farm, where he lived in the former house of A.A. Milne, to tell him the good news – I'd had a dream about water gods and knew this meant that he was destined to sail on to new musical continents.

He wasn't in. I thought I saw Princess Margaret through a window in the kitchen but it may have been a drunken mop propped against a wall. In the front garden were a lot of builders doing not much at all and on making polite inquiries as to his whereabouts I was told to fuck off or get my arse kicked. I thanked them politely for their invaluable assistance and wandered down the lane. My best recourse seemed to be alcohol and deep thought so I walked to the village pub, a little country place with a smiling barman and less chance of being told to fuck off, although he did ask my age as I looked very young. The gods of luck had pitied me. There, sitting quietly at a table sipping a pint of beer and smoking a cigarette was Brian Jones.

"I've just been to your house," I said.

"I'm not there," he said.

"So I came here."

"Which is where I am."

"I love the slide guitar on *Little Red Rooster*. It changed my life."

"How?"

"I went from being a skinny nerdy English kid to a log rolling warrior who could wrestle catfish the size of submarines."

"You're weird, kid."

"Thanks."

We sat quietly for a while, him sipping his beer and smoking, happily ignoring me, and me eating a bag of salt and vinegar crisps and drinking a pint of lager.

"Your builders are complete bastards," I said.

"I'm going to sack them," he said.

"You're starting another band," I said.

He looked at me, tired heavy eyes beneath a blonde freshly washed fringe.

"How do you know?"

"It was in my dream. Water gods and new musical horizons."

"Are you on something, or just fucked up in the head?"

"Just fucked up," I said.

"OK then. "

We sat in uneasy silence for a few minutes. I wanted to say something profound but all I could think of were the shapely legs of Rosie Banks and how I always tried to be behind her on the school bus so I could see the maddening delights beneath her skirt as she skipped upstairs. One day I would write an epic poem to her thighs.

"You know one of the worst things that's happened to me?" Brian suddenly asked.

"I dunno. Running out of cigarettes? Leaving the Stones?"

"No. Being rejected by monkeys."

"That would be tough."

"Barbary Macaques they're called. March 1967. Anita, Marianne Faithfull and I went to Gibraltar and I had the tape of my new work – the soundtrack for Anita's film *A Degree of*

Murder. I had this notion that the apes on the rock would appreciate my music."

"And why wouldn't they? What happened?"

"They were very quiet as we approached, all sitting on the rock looking at us. Very curious. Then I played the tape. They got all agitated, nervous, then they started screaming and jumping about and they all ran away. Why would they do that?"

"I guess the Gibraltar apes wouldn't be sophisticated enough to appreciate your music. Think about it. Gibraltar. Just a few fish and chip shops. And then down the road it's all sangria and bad flamenco. They weren't ready for you. What did you do?"

"I swore at the hairy little bastards. Then I broke down. Then I took a lot of acid."

"Sounds a very reasonable response. In the circumstances. I have to go now."

"Why?"

"I have a job delivering groceries on a bike and if I start hitching now I might just get back to London in time. Just so I know – you're only talking to me because you're drunk, right? Otherwise you wouldn't give me the time of day."

"Absolutely."

I got to the door and turned. His bowed head held all the shadowed sadness in the world but then he looked up and straight ahead and smiled like a doomed pixie. "It will all go wrong before it goes right," he said. Now, worlds later, I know he meant for both of us. Benefit of hindsight. Black dogs in the night. Chaos, carnage and confusion.

And I left. A few weeks later he was dead. Drowned. Probably murdered by the builder Frank Thorogood. Who was thoroughly bad. The water gods had decided to turn my dream on its head. I knew I would have to be very suspicious of dreams and gods and builders.

Chapter One: A Sexual Detour and a Crap Festival

Like all true odysseys, it begins with the mundane, and like most things, it began by accident. His smile was a rusty razor blade. His laugh a mouthful of splinters. His name was Mister Spick and he'd just offered me a job in Parks and Recreation in North London. How was I to know that Council workers were either insane or potential killers? How was I to know that I was to become an agent of global chaos.

We were young and hungry for everything. Somehow that desire insists you eat strange fruits and possibly destroy yourself. If so, the destruction would at best be a thing of terrible beauty. The summer of love became the autumn of madness. Death was in the air. Death was everywhere. I'd meet him often during the next few hectic brain altering years that would take me through the parks of North London, the deserts of Africa and the streets of Harlem in a determined bid to rid myself of sanity. Despite the annoying presence of the Reaper I wanted to be enlightened and start a revolution that would make the Garden of Eden look like a gas works. I was determined to spearhead a revolution that would change the world and alter human consciousness forever. Modesty does not sit well on the shoulders of the young.

There were a few good things already. I'd just left school and been to the Isle of Wight Festival where my Religious Studies teacher gave me life enhancing joyful sex in a tent while Tiny Tim sang 'There'll Always Be An England' in a high and wild trouser trembling falsetto. The sex was so good we didn't even need to take off our clothes the first time. She was twenty four and married. I was eighteen and ready to burn the world. Being a Religious Studies teacher, she made it her sacred duty to break as many of the Ten Commandments as were biologically possible in the tent with me that afternoon and thereafter. I was a willing cohort. We stopped short of murder, though microscopic organisms may have been squashed in the heat and delirium. We did it nineteen times in one weekend. God bless Religious Studies. Later on she would, in another religious act of love, appear from nowhere (actually she came down from Leeds, which to a Londoner is as good as nowhere at all) and save me from the teeth of a lunatic asylum with the generosity of her body. I was also sustained by the dream of University where I would learn how to be a clever bastard and know who Friedrich Nietzsche was and how to say his name properly. The other good thing was that I had an angel, a very big guy who hovered somewhere around my right shoulder. Sometimes he talked to me but I could never quite catch the words. It was a breeze caressing my ear. No matter what madness possesses me, no matter how far I push the boundaries, no matter what tide I decide to roll out with, I assumed he would always be there to protect me. Life makes fools of us all.

At the end of the Isle of Wight festival and with my glorious Religious Studies teacher who had given me the fizzbang of all educations, I was delirious with love and the erotic. This was just as well as it stopped me seeing in the full glare of reality what a hideous and shitty event the festival really was. The hippy dream, ever daft and delusional, collapsed in a heap of mung beans and poo, there being no proper toilets or sanitation. Being in a permanent sexual coma protected me from what I dimly perceived at the edge of my consciousness. Such as: going to what was laughingly called the toilet – a plank with holes every few feet placed over a ditch. One morning it broke and a dozen or so hippies fell into the feculent discharges of over half a million unwashed backsides. No one had the desire or the ability to rescue them.

There was also the whiff of violence underlying everything. Ten thousand radical dipshits camped outside on Desolation Hill and who then broke down the fences to get in, while half the people inside wanted by day two to get out. After a steamy twenty four hours in our tent, my Religious Studies nymphette and I went for a walk to the coast, after listening to Free sing 'Alright Now'. On a cliff top overlooking the sea we came upon a droopy hippy girl who seemed incapable of speech and a man whose head was painted silver, but who I recognised as a guitarist in the band, Hawkwind. He looked like Tin Man from *Somewhere Over the Rainbow.* I don't know what he'd taken but it seemed to have rearranged his brain cells into a flowery lobotomy.

I asked him if he was OK and he said, "Man, I don't know what who the thing, like the one or whatever, is with the feathers but it's, like, really spacey. It was, you know, something electrical or like a beastie thing with, what was it? Porridge or whatever. You know?"

"I know exactly what you mean," I said. It's never a good idea to attempt rational discussion with hippies who have taken a fridge load of bad acid and mescalin. And besides, I thought derangement would be an acceptable part of my revolution. I would have a whole island, perhaps the Isle of Wight, as a lunatic asylum, and brain-fried hippies could live there on nuts and berries and mescaline and could rub patchouli oil into each other's bits to cloak the collective BO. As a voyager in substance abuse I was in no position to condemn anyone.

One of the funniest things about the festival were the 'undercover' police officers, trying to find drug dealers and users. They stood out a mile. Even the way they walked was different. One man with a ridiculous curly wig and a kaftan, but wearing a pair of sensible brown leather Clark's shoes approached me, cleared his throat, and said in a slightly officious way, "Hey man, can I score?"

I asked him if he was a footballer and he looked slightly puzzled, and said, "I mean score some top grass, man."

I said I didn't work in the gardening trade and he moved on. Another police 'plant' approached me. He was smoking a senior service, which no self-respecting hippy degenerate would do, and I sold him a piece of mouldy cheese I'd had in my shoulder bag for a few weeks, for a pound, and told him it was top quality Lebanese. He never even arrested me. A young police woman, with kohl making her eyes water badly, and wearing a pair of hot pants made for someone three sizes smaller than her, later asked where she could score some acid. I pretended I was deaf and started signing gibberish and she made a valiant attempt to respond, but when my gestures became slightly obscene she walked away.

And speaking of substance abuse I stood at the front when Jimi Hendrix played what was his last full concert. He was already late on and a lot of people booed. He spent a lot of time talking to his roadies rather than playing. The man looked ill. I'd seen him play a few years before when his every gesture and note detonated electrical storms, but he was now a pale shadow of his former self, a brightly plumaged wounded bird who had two weeks to live. The day after the festival finished, when all that remained were windblown dreams, mountains of rubbish, and a potpourri of offal and faeces and urine, I watched someone completely off his head running around the broken desolate stage waving a sword like a lobotomised samurai. This was apparently Hendrix's manager at the time – it didn't augur well for the guitarist's business interests. He's probably now a window cleaner in Bognor.

Chapter Two: Mad, Bad and Dangerous

The Parks crew were knights of the roads and keepers of the sacred green. We rocked in ancient charioteering lorries along the North Circular Road like ragged warriors, gloved and wellingtoned in rain, skinny legged and pot-bellied in heat, with our rusty scythes and our petrol driven mowers and other accoutrements of death, ready to battle with the Gothic hordes of bramble, the heathen nettles, unruly branches and metropolis of weeds that gave us the very work that ensured their destruction. The lorries would scourge Enfield and Edmonton, Southgate, Oakwood, Trent Park, Barnet and Winchmore Hill, work their way across the borders to the uncivilized wastelands of Hornsey and Wood Green, cutting, slicing and laying waste the green and brown. A lot of tea was drunk. A lot of arses scratched. A lot of exotic things smoked. A lot of time usefully wasted. I was now with the rejects, rebels and the downright insane of society – the people nobody else would employ. The council was a refuge for lost souls. I had no idea it would change my life forever.

Terry was a sixteen year old teddy boy with greased blonde curls and the face of a stupid angel. Small, packed with muscle, toxic eyes that glittered violence. Later in life his hobbies would include rape and torturing rodents. In an act of wilful malice by the goblin who controlled Parks and Recreation I was frequently paired with Terry. The lorry would unload us and our mowers on some patch of green scrub in a suburb and as soon as it chugged off Terry would square up to me and say "Wanna fight?" "No," I'd say, and he'd jump on me and begin a roly-poly fight, getting me in arm locks and leg locks and head locks and sometimes just for the fun of it seeing how far it would bend before my spine snapped. I'd desperately think of something to say that would stop him, so that I could lay back on the grass and let my bones crack back into place and watch clouds. Watching clouds is all I wanted to do. Then he'd start again but eventually we'd chug the mowers alive, do a few minutes work and the lorry would pick us up. My angel was clearly on a tea break. I had bruises on my bruises. My bones hooped and creaked.

It was like being with a wired chimpanzee, never knowing when he would turn on me. The very air around him was menacing. He embodied the violence of genuine stupidity. I finally found a way of getting him onside. He loved Eddie Cochran. I told him I played guitar and could teach him to play Eddie Cochran songs. I could see the madness relax behind his eyes, as he imagined himself in front of a mirror, playing guitar and perfecting a rockabilly sneer.

"Is it hard?" he asked, sensing a trap.

I told him it was as hard as he wanted it to be. That you could learn a few chords fairly quickly and many rock songs only had three chords. It never materialised, of course, he was too splintered to learn anything, but whenever the red mist came over him, which was often, I'd dangle the carrot of three chords and a rock and roll dream before him and he'd haze over long enough for the heat in him to melt.

One morning Terry dropped me in it so far I could almost hear the ambulance siren.

Brian had great dark, moist, pouchy bags under his eyes that had lives of their own. There was a galaxy of depressing experience in those bags. They weighed so much they gave him a stoop. You could still see them through the large shades he sometimes wore to keep the world at bay, and to stop the light disturbing his misery. He had a hellish comb-over – a few dark strands of hair that flopped across his dome like wilted centipedes. He chain smoked and wore big floppy leather boots like Harold Steptoe. He lived under a curse and murdered people in his dreams, sometimes the same people over and over, especially his wife who left him for a carpet fitter in Southgate. His demons rarely let him be. He was also epileptic. He sat in the tea room like a depressed gargoyle.

"Steve sez you're a mad eppy," Terry said to Brian, nodding at me, smirking. "'Bin telling everyone round the parks."

The atmosphere chilled a thousand degrees. Cracked stained mugs quivered between hand and lip. Eyes swivelled to

Brian, who looked at me and took off his shades, his eyes black olive pips, the great wet bags swelling with violence.

I wished Terry dead and thought quickly.

Brian was already out of his seat, his knuckles white.

"If anyone's been spreading it round the council I'm a madman I'll fucking kill 'em," he said. Everyone knew he meant it. It was a scarily short route from the thought to the deed. Consequences of actions never appeared on his radar. He stepped towards me. "You saying I'm a madman, I'll kill ya'."

"Course I didn't," swallowing my fear and trying to lighten the atmosphere.

He looked at me like a broken machine. "Say I'm a madman round the council I'll kill you," he repeated unnecessarily.

"Why would I? I mean, do I look like someone who'd do that?"

Clearly I did because Brian took a step forward, the bags under his eyes trembling like bruised harpies. Terry was smirking and enjoying the whole prospect of slaughter in the tea room. Everyone else was silent.

"Terry's winding you up, Brian. Can't you see that? Look how he's laughing. He just wants to see if you'll believe him."

A frown appeared on Brian's forehead, as if he was trying to solve a difficult calculus. He looked at Terry, at me, then back at Terry.

"'E did. E' told everyone you was a cracked eppy nutter," said Terry.

"What would be the point, Brian?" I said, starting to sweat, "I don't even know you. Why would I want to make life difficult for you? Ask anyone here if they think I'm the sort of bloke would do that." Everyone looked neutral and said nothing. There was blood in the air. They weren't going to jeopardise it by defending the innocent. Thanks, fellas. I was getting desperate. "Brian, I swear I did not say anything about you to anyone. I swear."

Brian reeled under the moral strain of choice. Kill me or not. Eventually the strain took its toll and he decided to kill me. He picked up a rusty knife from the table, but my angel intervened and the door opened and George the superintendent entered. The lorries were there to take us out. Brian backed off and sat down heavily. "Say I'm a madman round the council I'll kill 'ya," he said wearily. My pulses slowed. I thanked the faint rustle of wings at my right shoulder.

Afterwards I always made sure I was a few steps away from Brian, and that I never got in range when he held a rake or any sort of gardening weapon. A month later it all hit the fan, or, to be precise, it hit the door. We got our wages in a little brown packet every Thursday evening. There'd been a cock up and Brian's wages weren't there. George promised he'd take them to Brian's house himself later that evening. He didn't. The next morning we were hanging around outside waiting for our daily orders from Dennis the Assistant Super.

"Fucking 'ell," said someone. I looked around. Striding purposefully and with a speed he never showed during work, Brian was approaching holding a large axe in front of him. He had his shades and Steptoe boots on. Dennis came out of the parks building, smiling nervously and lighting his pipe. The smile froze when he saw Brian approaching. The pipe fell with a clunk and Dennis ran back into the office and shut the door. Brian was there. He banged on the door.

"Where's me wages?" he bellowed.

Dennis made the foolish mistake of not answering.

"I saw you go in, Den. Where's me wages. Where's George?" Not a peep.

The axe splintered the door in two large swipes and would have splintered Dennis in one had he not been able to wriggle through the lavatory window, and was now belting it hotfoot across the park. By the time Brian had axed the desk to death the police and an ambulance arrived. It took four coppers to get Brian on the floor and the axe out of his paws. They cuffed and cautioned him and minutes later he was whisked away.

"You was right. E's a fucking mad eppy," said Terry to me, forgetting that he'd made it all up.

Excitement over. There was tea to be drunk. Arses to be scratched. Things to be smoked. Even a bit of work to be done.

A few weeks later we found out that Brian was in the Maudsley psychiatric hospital in South London. It was bad enough being crazy, but to be in South London was infinitely worse. Little did I know I'd be with the loony tunes myself in the not too distant future.

Chapter Three: Dennis, Lucky, Julie and George

Dennis smoked a pipe, had crinkly hair like Rupert Davies as Inspector Maigret, short stocky legs and tried not to look terrified by smiling constantly, which made him look more terrified. He walked like a duck. Dennis had two big problems. His wife and his job. He desperately wanted a friend and, unfortunately, I was the chosen one. It was a bad choice. If I'd been his friend I could have told him that.

Dennis was in his mid forties and his wife, Julie, was twenty one. They lived in a house in the park at reduced rent. Every lunchtime Julie brought Den's sandwiches up to the cabin. We would all troop outside to watch as she wore the shortest skirts in the world, no more than a ribbon, and had smooth creamy legs and a peachy little arse. A tight blouse showed off pert tits like upturned champagne glasses. Poor Den would smile nervously, knock out his pipe again and again and try not to notice that every cretinous slob and psycho on the payroll drooled with boiling lust as she walked by. We ached with longing. Every mindless nobhead who worked there wanted to fuck her, and the worst wanted to do a hell of a lot more. Disho, a long haired weirdo in combat fatigues, would lick out his yoghurt pot so vehemently when Julie came up that the fur on his tongue scraped off and he had to take antibiotics. Old Belcher, a guy with irritable bowel and an ulcer, had to swallow a bucket of rennies to calm his stomach. Mick the Dick disappeared in the mowing shed for a quick wank. It was a mystery to me why Den let her do it. Did he enjoy showing her off? Was he a raving masochist? Was he truly an innocent and didn't realise the cauldron of worms her foxy little body unleashed every lunchtime?

Dennis felt passed over. He thought he should have been made Superintendent of Oakwood Park and not George. Julie felt he should be Super too and never missed an opportunity to remind him, which made him worse. The bitterer he became the more he smiled and clenched his pipe until one of his front teeth cracked off. He desperately needed someone to talk to, but given that most conversation in the cabin consisted of grunts and farts, tea slurping competitions, discussions about various bits of Julie and what everyone would like to do to them, and occasional outbursts of violent threats, Dennis was short on intelligent and sympathetic counsel.

"You're not like them," he said to me.

And so it was I found myself invited to dinner. I was given a schooner of sherry and introduced to Lucky the dog, who had tics, a broken leg and had just lost an eye on a rose bush and wore a plastic bucket on his head to stop him tearing at the stitches. I quickly realised Lucky was the child they couldn't have. Something desperate in their love for him. This seemed to create a suicidal impulse in Lucky.

Dinner turned out to be sandwiches in the local pub. After his fourth pint the floodgates opened in Dennis. How he'd been passed over. How George didn't deserve to be Super. How Dennis had always tried to be fair to the blokes. How he knew they laughed at him, and mocked his constipated duck walk. How wonderful it was to have Julie supporting him in his professional crisis. How she was a class above everyone and how lucky he was that she loved him so much. How lucky they were to have Lucky. Then he put his head on my shoulder and had a little sob. Things seemed to be getting out of hand when he started rubbing his foot up and down the back of my leg. Jesus H. Christ, I liked Dennis, but I wasn't going to end up giving him a sympathy fuck. Where would he put his pipe? I suddenly realised the angle was all wrong, unless Den's leg was triple jointed. It was Julie sitting facing me, looking sympathetically wifely at Den as he sobbed, but with her foot now wedged in my crotch and the big toe doing amazing things to my cock. She really knew how to work that toe. The table was lifting slightly and the mustard in my ham sandwich was burning my throat. I couldn't swallow.

"You're not like them," Den said, and wittered on about how glad he was to meet someone intelligent, someone who could understand, someone he could trust. A friend.

I had Den slobbering in my ear, his randy little wife masturbating me with her toe and a ham and mustard sandwich stuck in my mouth. No wonder Lucky was so accident prone living with all these contradictions.

An hour later Den was sprawled on his kitchen floor drinking cooking sherry from the bottle and kissing Lucky, who had caught his one good front paw in a mouse trap. I was desperately trying to leave, but it was difficult because Julie was standing next to me with one hand down my pants fondling my arse like it was a plum she was sizing up at the grocers.

"It means so much to us you coming out to dinner," she said, smiling up at me and nestling a breast under my armpit. "And you can be a real friend to Den at work. He needs one. So do I."

"I love you," said Den to poor Lucky, who looked up at me miserably with his one good eye. We were both hooked in to somewhere we didn't want to be. It was a house of desolation and despair.

Half an hour later I escaped when Julie took a toilet break from molesting me and a barely conscious Den had Lucky in a half nelson embrace of smothering, desperate love.

The next day I joined the enemy, as far as Dennis was concerned, so I was spared the ordeal of another dinner invitation. George came into the tea room and said "I want to see you for a minute." All eyes were on me. Was it punishment, or worse, promotion? Promotion would mean easier work, but the gang would hate you. You'd become a brown-nosing sneak renegade, an arse frumping apostasy no longer welcome in the cold, cheerless hostility of the filthy tea room.

My worst fears were realised. I sat in the van, George smiled at me from the driver's seat. He had the face of a healthy, tanned gerbil, all teeth and cheeks. Small, with industrial energy, busy little legs and mad wavy hair. "You seem like you got a brain," he said. "You'll be coming out in the van with me for a while." I was doomed. First persecuted by the love of Dennis and his frisky wife, now favoured by the Superintendent himself.

Going out in the van with George meant becoming Keeper of many secrets and getting a hell of a lot of free vegetables. Every day he would stop at a house and disappear inside for half an hour. He'd come out and say "Do you like mushrooms?" and give me a huge basket of them. The next day it would be a different house and I'd get a sweet smelling bunch of fresh carrots. The next day another house and onions. Once I got a sack of artichokes. That must have been a good session. My family had never eaten so healthily. I never saw the women, and I never knew where the vegetables came from, perhaps they were part of the encounter, but I knew to keep my mouth shut. I wondered where he met the women in the first place. There seemed to be a different house every day. Rumour was that although he had left his wife she still spat razor blades. He rarely saw his daughter and when someone mentioned her a look of infinite pain shadowed his face.

Old George seemed to have a good routine. And a lot of energy. So it came as a surprise when I arrived at work one morning and Den came out, for once unsmiling, shocked to the bone, his unlit pipe in his hand, and hissed, "George topped himself. They found him in the mower shed this morning. He swallowed a whole bottle of rat poison. He was surrounded by fresh vegetables."

It was the end of my cushy days in the van and my mum had to start buying vegetables again. And now Dennis was Acting Superintendent perhaps he wouldn't covet my friendship, and Julie would calm down, and Lucky would get through a week without nearly killing himself. And I could get back to the serious business of life and enlightenment and thinking about the revolution I wanted to start. The revolution would surely be accompanied by Ron Wood on bottleneck guitar and Peter Green singing sweet blues.

A Short Interlude on the Mysteries of the Internal Combustion Engine

My driving instructor had one glass eye. Two would have been fatal but one was bad enough, because it meant he turned his head sideways to see through the windscreen properly, and I adopted the same habit, which has given me many a neck ache down the years, and many a near miss with fatal car crashes. My first car was a Rover 90 that I bought from a man in a back street in Shoreditch for twenty five pounds. It was beautiful with a continuous leather seat in the front for driver and passenger, and enough chrome to build an aeroplane. I felt like a king. The only problem with this magnificent beast was that you could only start it with a large metal starting handle that you had to fit in the front grille to turn the engine over. It was impossible for a weedy seventeen-year-old to do, especially one who had failed technical drawing three times at school. I just couldn't do it, and even if I did manage to grind the handle around once it would kick back like a neanderthal mule with a hangover, and nearly break my wrist. So the only way I could take my girlfriend out in this car was to get my Dad to start the car at home, and either keep it running while we sat in a country pub drinking cider, or stop it and then then find a phone box and ring my Dad to drive wherever we were and start Rover for me. Bless him, he did this numerous times. My Uncle also towed me with his scrap metal lorry when I accidentally reversed into a ditch, but he was drunk and forgot to untie me so Rover was dragged all the way home with me shouting behind the wheel and my girlfriend saying she never wanted to see me again.

My second car I bought for a hefty eighty pounds from a man who met me in a public car park. It was a green mini estate and looked in pretty good shape. He took the money and gave me the log book and keys and drove off in his own car. The crucial thing he failed to tell me was that the car didn't work. I consoled myself with the thought that the paintwork was nice and shiny. I left the car and got a few mates to come and help me push it home. We parked it on the road at the back of the house.

It stayed there for six months, completely inanimate, but the paintwork still looked good. Finally my Dad said "If that car isn't gone by Sunday I'll take action."

When I came home from an all night party on Sunday morning a neighbour was out front and he said, with no little awe in his voice: "Your Dad did the whole thing in an hour with just a hacksaw. Amazing."

I went round the back and there was a skip with my mini estate cut cleanly in half. My Dad was a man of his word. I noticed that the whole of the underside of the car had been reinforced with flattened Heinz Bean tins, so maybe it was just as well it didn't go or the first time I put my foot down it would have gone through the floor, like a Fred Flintstone car.

My third car was another mini. Black with smoked windows. I loved that car. The only problem was that the brakes didn't work at all and I couldn't afford to get them fixed, so there was a lot of gear crunching and use of hand braking. I also perfected a technique of driving very slowly driving into walls and trees as a way of stopping. It finally came to an end when I drove to Ross on Wye with a friend, Paul, to see some girls we'd met at a Pontins Holiday camp the summer before. All was going well until we went down a steep hill and I couldn't get in a lower gear and the handbrake went on strike. I started to make an inventory of all the things I hadn't yet done in life, such as: have sex in an aeroplane; have sex in a car; have sex on a beach; have sex in a wardrobe; have sex in a coffin; have sex in a jacuzzi; have sex anywhere (I was still young and uninitiated). I'd just moved on from sex in my farewell to life when there was an almighty whumpf as we careered off the road, through a hedge and into a muddy field. The mud slowed us down with a jerk that bounced us both up to the roof and back. When my head cleared I was aware of a pair of large sad eyes looking at me through the window. A very beautiful cow gently chewing whatever cows chew.

We donated the car to the cows and hitchhiked home. When the police came round a week later I said the car had been stolen and they believed me.

My next car was a Ford Anglia with a fan belt made of a pair of tights borrowed from my Auntie Lil. It was a fine little car but had a habit of jumping a gear and lurching forward at inopportune moments. I went to Enfield Town one night to my favourite folk club, a small room off a bar where you could see amazing musicians. One night Alexis Korner played. He was the grandfather of blues in England and without him there would be no Rolling Stones, no Free. Anyone who was anyone in the blues scene played with him at some point. I loved his gravelly, Gitane-stained voice and soulful guitar playing. And here he was in a small bar at the backside of a North London pub playing to a handful of people, me at the front. When he wasn't singing he was smoking. After his set I had a glass of white wine with him and we talked about favourite blues singers. When he said he had to go I offered him a lift to the station, but he told me he had Bella, his old blue Cortina, and we shook hands. Outside I was still thinking of the chord sequence in one of his songs as I put my old Anglia into gear and it lurched forward several feet and smashed into the front of an old blue Cortina.

Bella was now officially fucked. I could see that. I reversed, dragging a bit of Bella's front bumper with me, and wondered what to do. In a sense it was an honour to have wrecked the car of Britain's best blues man, but the downside was he might hate me for the rest of his life. I had twenty pounds in my wallet that I was saving for a new Yamaha acoustic guitar. I put it in an old envelope and fixed it behind Bella's windscreen wiper and went home. I felt bad but then I often felt bad about things I'd done.

Two weeks later I got a letter and inside a short handwritten note: *You bastard. Thanks for the twenty quid.* Stupidly the envelope I'd put the money in had my name and address on it. I decided a life of crime wasn't waiting for me. I would rob a jeweller's and then probably leave a calling card.

There is a whole life story in cars.

Chapter Four: God Begins Destroying My Friends

By 1971 God had made a kaleidoscopic comeback. The bastard was everywhere. Christianity, Divine Light Mission, the giggling Maharishi, Ali Baba and his brother Meher Baba, the Zen of everything from washing machines to herpes and haemorrhoids, Jesus freaks, Buddhism (I know there's no god in it but Buddha was sort of worshipped by a lot of people), the scary Hare Krishna lot, the Orange people. Everyone was getting religion – George Harrison, Bob Dylan, Charlie Manson, me. I decided I was Jesus Christ but had great difficulty persuading other people to accept this, except for those who thought the Lord was in everyone, and they didn't count. You can't have a whole world of Messiahs. Even at rock concerts there was a nutter called Jesus who would start off just listening, then as more and more cells dissolved in his brain he'd dance and gyrate and fling off his clothes and always end up glistening with sweat and bollock naked. If you sat near him you risked either drowning or getting an eye knocked out by a swinging hippy pendulum todger.

I thought there would be a place for God in the revolution I was vaguely plotting. I had no idea how dangerous He was, especially when he appeared in the parks, and decided to take down a few of my friends.

Like many others I was a religious tart. I slept with the lot and never took precautions. The only one I merely flirted with was the Hare Krishna lot. They would be bop down Oxford Street like punk rock Mohicans shouting 'Hairy Krishna Hairy Krishna Krishna Krishna Hairy Hairy' (which made it easy to learn the words and suggests it was a faith for those with learning difficulties) tinkling their bells and playing bongos very badly. They invited me to their house in Museum Street and gave me a bowl of chick peas and a girl said she would have sacred sex with me all night. All I had to do in return was shave my head, wear a yellow frock and devote the rest of my life to Krishna. I didn't even have to learn to play the bongos badly. A bargain for salvation to many, I suppose, but to me a lethal dose. They turned nasty when I said I had a job to do in the parks and after that was going to university to learn to be a clever bastard. In fact they suddenly seemed more like young Nazis and for a while I thought they wouldn't let me go, but I managed to jostle my way through a lot of cheesecloth and incense fumes and threatening looks and abuse to the front door and escape into the pure filth of London.

My great friend John Logan and I had been given the job of mowing the grass verges in a very long and posh road. It was a bastard of a job because I had a dippy mower that kept veering to the right and scraping the paint off cars on the road as I struggled to correct it. After about three minutes of sweating labour I'd had enough and sat down to smoke a Bensons. John joined me and we left our mowers chugging in the hope they would run out of petrol. John was musical, impish, and we'd both gotten into a lot of trouble at school. We both liked drugs and Tommy Cooper and hated being a member of anything, including the human race. He looked like Bob Dylan from the Blonde on Blonde cover, an album we both revered as sacred. 'Visions of Johanna' seemed proof there was a god. "Jewels and binoculars hang from the head of the mule. But these visions of Johanna, they make it all seem so cruel" seemed to me the height of wisdom, and still does, even though I don't have a clue what it means. I had long hair too and looked like a King Charles spaniel bitch. We took LSD once and ended up high in a tree in Trent Park at three in the morning, having covered ourselves in brylcreem, and I kept forgetting my name. John would make suggestions – "Boom. Accident. Zeus. Hartleypool. Gravity. Jelly. Flange. Chunder. Heliotrope. Vest." Each seemed more hilarious than the last and I wanted to be called by them all. Great as LSD was, the sense of humour suffers arrested development. When the Park Keeper stumbled on our babbling madness the next morning I tried to explain it was fine because we worked for the council and were just doing overtime. The fact that I had somehow lost my trousers and had a hydrangea in my hair and John was sitting in a pond discussing something of great philosophical importance with a frog failed to convince. We escaped when a giant eagle swooped low and beckoned us onto her fine scalloped wings. I smell now the kill fresh on her claws, the plangent air as she gained speed and elevation, the good smell of feathered life and the moon like a weeping sulphurous eye before dawn as she took us home, which is finally where everyone wants to go. Then we listened to the Beatles *White Album* and tried to discern secret messages about revolution and God until we fell into giggling unconsciousness.

John and I sat on the kerb listening to our wheezing motors and he said we ought to go to the Divine Light Mission meeting at Haringey Dog Track that evening. Guru Maharaj Ji himself would be there. I'd been to DLM meetings before but had never seen the Boy Wonder himself, and was curious. We gave two little kids a bob each to mow the verges for us while we discussed God and Truth and India and drugs and different kinds of tits. I had only just embraced Christianity and gotten over the painful realisation that I might not be the Messiah, but if God was all knowing he wouldn't mind if I joined another lot as well. It was all one, according to George Harrison and Buddha and my Gran, who was fond of saying "Everything is crap." Half an hour later the lorry arrived. Jim the blow-up man, a new supervisor, and so called because he had a pimple on his bald head that looked like a nippled air valve, looked at us accusingly. What was his problem?

"Well?" He asked.

"Yes, I'm fine. Thanks for asking. And you?" I replied.

The teat on his dome flushed scarlet. I saw a little fart of steam jet from it. "I mean: Well, what the fuck are you doing?"

"We're just having a fag break."

"A fag break. A fucking fag break. Where's the fucking mowers?"

We both looked around. Shit. The mowers had gone. The kids had gone. The grass verges had wobbly lines that ended at the pavement, then nothing. We got on the lorry and drove around a bit, but they'd vanished. This could mean the sack. Luckily, one of the little kids sliced off a toe in the mower, and the hospital contacted Parks and Recreation, and the mowers were returned. Jim was disappointed. He hated us. We were young, irresponsible, and were obviously close to God, and about to get closer.

There was a big crowd already when we arrived at Haringey Dog Track. Divine Light Mission had grown enormously in a short time, borne in on a broad wind of pop music, flower power, drugs, and a vague yearning for something else. DLM had big gatherings in London that were like Billy Graham revival meetings, then on the interest generated by these it would have numerous offshoot meetings in private houses in the suburbs. There was one near where I lived in Palmers Green. About a dozen of us sat cross-legged on the carpet before a smiling and sometimes giggling Indian who spent up to six hours telling us very little. Mostly, it was that the world was an illusion and all that mattered was getting the 'knowledge'; at the end of the session he would choose a few lucky souls to receive the 'knowledge.' As a corporate religion it was stupendously successful, because an army of devotees of DLM were conscripted as worker ants. DLM started to buy up properties all over London, move in followers who then repaired and decorated the houses for nothing, and which were then sold at a profit. The dosh was rolling in. It must be wonderful to be so spiritually elevated that you can make people give up all their money and possessions and devote their whole lives to making you richer, and for it to mean absolutely nothing to you. This is true enlightenment.

At the heart of DLM was the Holy family, and at the heart of that Guru Maharaj Ji himself, a chubby teenager in white pyjamas with a garland of flowers around his neck and black greasy hair. He looked like a mutated Roy Orbison. I guess he was chubby because he didn't have much exercise. A brand new white Rolls Royce would take him everywhere and all he had to do was walk from the car to the stage and then sit there for a few hours telling us that the world was an illusion. His Rolls Royce was an illusion, his Bentley was an illusion. All the Rollers he had given to his brothers and his Mum were illusions. All his properties over the world and his mansion in India were illusions. Sometimes it was difficult not to think that it might be nice to drive around in a big shiny illusion oneself, but such worldly thoughts meant that, unlike Guru Maharaj Ji, we were not yet enlightened. We all adored him for being so spiritual.

The rollers were already lined up outside, so John and I trooped in and sat cross-legged on the floor. A lot of smiling Indians wearing garlands of flowers talked devotedly about Guru Maharaj Ji, who sat on a throne surrounded by flowers. It was starting to look more like Gardeners World than heaven and everyone's hay fever was going through the roof. Eventually he spoke himself for about five hours about how the world was an illusion and all that mattered was getting the Knowledge. John was chosen to get the Knowledge that night. I went to the front of the stage and said I wanted it too, but a smiling Indian covered in flowers said the fact that I was asking showed I wasn't yet ready. Of course I'm fucking ready, I thought. Why else would I spend five hours listening to a load of old twaddle if I wasn't ready to be fucking enlightened? And I wanted my own roller to show that it meant nothing to me. I thought of just pushing my way to the back of the stage and saying I had been chosen but a divine bouncer stopped me with his enormous belly and shunted me back to join the unenlightened throng.

John came out about an hour later and said his third eye had been opened. I told him he'd look pretty silly if he had to wear glasses. He said it was all to do with the Knowledge he'd received, which was a sacred secret he could never reveal to a living soul. We went to the Cock Tavern in Palmers Green to celebrate the opening of his third eye and after four pints of lager, some speed and a joint we smoked in the toilet he seemed to forget about the sacred secret and told me what the Knowledge was. You pinched your eyes together with the first and third finger of your right hand and put the index finger on your forehead and after a few seconds you saw a white light. That was your third eye opening. It took some people years to receive the Knowledge. It took me five minutes in the pub with my mate. You could tell people who'd received the Knowledge because they all looked a bit cross eyed. Then John dropped his bombshell. He was leaving the parks and going to live in a Divine Light Mission house in Wood Green and devote his life to Guru Maharaj Ji.

The next time I saw him was three months later in hospital. He was strapped up in bed, both legs shattered. He said he'd been working on the roof of a DLM three storey house, replacing tiles and cleaning the guttering, when he suddenly had a revelation – that Guru Maharaj Ji wanted him to show the full extent of his love for him. All he could think to do was walk off the roof, which is what he did. He looked different. Not just the mangled legs, but something essential had been extinguished. The long curls had gone. The impish eyes no longer danced. His skin looked waxy. I don't think Guru Maharaj Ji ever came to see him, or even sent him a Get Well card. I saw John once more, a few years later, when he'd just come out of a loony tunes hospital. He said someone had put a clock in his head and if it ever stopped the world would end, and it started to drive him mad. We had a drink but the buzz was gone. I suggested he get a job in the parks again but he said they were all mad. The blind leading the blind leading the blind.

Chapter Five: He Do the Dead in Different Voices

Peter was my brother and nemesis. A nascent angel, starlit and maddened by light, he travelled far and never took hostages. It was all or nothing. You are with me or you are against me. He created an abundant harvest of chaos and madness and misery and laughter. An Icarus of the 1970s. He would be John of Patmos in the revolution which would surely come once I'd hammered out the details.

We met in Pymmes Park, he looking for work, and recognising someone who was both a seeker of truth and a freak, the council immediately employed him. He was twenty two, an excellent slide guitarist, and married to a bus conductress, a clippie called Gail, who had such big tits that he said he was often at a loss to know what to do with them. We both loved Peter Green's guitar playing, the way he coaxed and bent strings, and could take the heat out of electric notes so that they soften you up, then break your heart. And a sweet, lazy, nicotine voice. When he sang "Yet somehow I wish I'd never been born" you knew he meant it.

England had awoken from a long dream of post war blues and everywhere people were learning to talk. I felt my mouth was a small bird wanting to sing and fly. Peter said he wasn't sure if he wanted to own the whole world or renounce it, and he felt that if he played his guitar fast enough he would disappear and find himself in some other universe. He'd started reading the Bible and quoted Jeremiah chapter ten where it says "Everyone is senseless and without knowledge" and we agreed that this just about summed up everyone we knew. In chapter twenty it says "I will make you a terror to yourself and all your friends." Peter thought this might happen to him, especially as the song 'Hellhound on my Trail' kept blasting at him from nowhere, and which clearly meant someone was out to get him. Maybe Satan himself. The Old Testament suited our apocalyptic sense of a bright but exploding world and, like all young people, a mythic sense of ourselves. The Old Testament was to become the narrative of our lives. Every moment dripped with foreboding and hidden significance. He said most people talk about nothing. I said I loved talking about nothing because I knew so much about it.

On Peter's first day at work, Dennis, now back as Assistant, gave us a clearance job. These were the worst. You were taken somewhere in the jungle of suburbia, explorers in unknown territory, with only a scythe, a spade, industrial shears, and what remained of your wits to hack your way back to civilization. We were at the back of a private hospital. A large area had been allowed to grow unfettered for years – a tangle of blackberry thorn, nettle, thistle and stubborn briar. Hippies all say they love nature, but they didn't have to do clearance jobs. Nature is intractable and frighteningly indifferent. We could die in this wilderness. If you didn't have gloves you were lost. The nails would go, the fingers would bleed and swell and ache and get bitten by the mysterious iniquities that lived in the wilderness. For a good guitarist like Peter and an average one like me it was the death of music. The universe was a long train we could ride to anywhere but there were malevolent forces too in the dark heart of clearance jobs.

Peter wasn't used to getting up at 6.30 am so he decided to have a rest and smoke a few roll ups before actually commencing work. I got right in. Cut, hack, slash. The air was gorged with pollen, chopped leaves, and the angry buzz of things disturbed. I enjoyed this sort of intense sweat sometimes. It cleared out some of the brain clutter and opened spaces for dreams. I came upon a gobliney briar that refused to budge. I slashed and hacked and pulled but it was mulishly stubborn. The roots went down to Australia. I decided that the rest of my life would be determined by this moment. I would get the bastard out or bust. I started digging around it. Peter was giving a lengthy discourse on the resurrection of Lazarus. "'And he that was dead came forth, bound hand and foot with graveclothes: and his face was bound about with a napkin…' He brings him back to life to increase the faith of his followers. And to show what will happen on the last day."

I could see this mummified, partly decaying figure staggering out of a tomb. It seemed more like a horror film than a religion.

"The problem is that Christianity becomes Zombieism," I said.

Peter looked at me. "In my father's house there are many mansions," he said.

"What's that got to do with it?"

"Everything. There must have been a special place where Lazarus was during the four days when he was dead. But is it exactly the same self? Because now, he's had the experience of death – the only person ever to know death and come back. Or was that knowledge extinguished?"

"You could remake the New Testament as a horror film," I said, yanking at the bastard briar.

"What?"

"Jesus as a sort of mad Frankenstein who brings back the dead. Call it Gospel of the Evil Dead. Zombies of Zion. Or Testament of Zombies. Bible of the Body Snatchers. All these undead people, maybe some of them don't even want to come back and the disciples have to start killing them all again to restore the balance of nature, but Jesus has gone off on one and can't stop bringing back the dead. And that's why they crucify him in the end. 'Cos people can't get rid of their unwanted family members. The bastards just keep coming back."

"That might be blasphemous," said Peter.

Sod Lazarus – I'd finally got the better of the briar. I could feel its roots budge. I gave one final yank and pulled as hard as I could. It came out bringing half the world with it. I looked at the fruits of my labour. What I saw gave me one of the biggest shocks of my life. I was so aghast my legs gave way and I thumped heavily to the ground. I sat pointing, my mouth opening and closing like a fish. Peter looked up and the roll up fell from his mouth.

"Jesus H Christ," we both said.

There was a body. It sat looking at us, even though it had no eyes, just a sort of dried out jellified gunge in each of the sockets. It had been hidden by the briar, and from waist down it was covered in earth and weed, the legs straight out. I could see that it had been lying down, but that a few fierce thistles had grown and slowly raised the trunk and head. One of the thistles had actually grown through the chest, and looked like a plumed Viking helmet where the heart should be.

"Who is he?" I asked no one in particular. It was a stupid question.

"How do you know it's a he?" Peter asked.

"No tits."

"But the tits probably just moulded away. Or maybe she was flat chested."

Curiosity slowly overcame fear and revulsion. Peter made two roll ups and we smoked them, watching our new companion.

"I think it's too late for him to be resurrected," I said.

"Or her."

Peter went closer. He sniffed. There was no repulsive smell. Who was it? How long had it been there?

"You reckon it was murdered?"

"Hardly seems plausible that it crawled into a nest of thorns and briars and suddenly died of natural causes."

"We ought to give it a name."

"Dave," I said.

"You're sure it's a bloke?"

"It is now."

We had a good look around Dave, searching for personal possessions, or a weapon. On one arm was a faded piece of blue and white check material. The head was leaning back slightly, the mouth open in a macabre grin, the skin like burnt leather. Peter had a bottle of Fanta. He held it above Dave's head and poured some into the open mouth. It was extraordinary. Leaks started all over the chest and little bubbles of Fanta appeared.

"We should do something," I said.

"We are doing something."

The hair was short and filthy, with a few bugs and beetles scuttling about.

"We should have called him Lazarus," said Peter.

"We can't. He's Dave. He'll get confused if we start chopping and changing his identity."

Peter had a little Bible with him and he started reading a few things, including "Ashes to ashes, dust to dust...all flesh is grass..." I remembered a line from Whitman. "Grass is the beautiful uncut hair of graves." Then Peter sat in the lotus position facing Dave and started humming, his eyes closed.

"What are you doing?" I asked.

"Communing. I'm trying to connect with Dave's consciousness."

I looked at the tattered dried out remains of Dave's skull. This would be a tough one. Ten minutes later I asked Peter if he was picking up anything. He said he was getting a powerful image of a large one-eyed woman wearing red knickers, also a squirrel and a tub of margarine. What the hell had Dave been up to? We spent another ruminative six hours speculating on the possible map of Dave's life and when Jim the blow-up man arrived in the lorry I realised I'd be quite sad to leave him. We started loading our instruments of death on the lorry. Jim was furious. The valve on his head was practically gushing steam.

"Two of you and look, you've hardly done nothing."

"Three of us," corrected Peter.

"Us two and Dave," I said.

"You two are fucking weird. Who's Dave?"

"He's in the bushes."

"What – you mean a fucking pervert?"

"No. He's too quiet for that," I said. "He could have been a librarian or something. Maybe an agricultural surveyor. Anyway, we couldn't just carry on working and ignore him. It would have been rude."

Jim got out of the lorry, his temper inflaming his blood. He went to the bushes, then reeled back white as a zombie himself.

"There's a dead person there. A fucking corpse!"

"I don't think he does much fucking these days. His name's Dave."

"What happened?"

"We just found him."

"When?"

"This morning."

"You spent all fucking day with a corpse? What you been doing with it?"

"Peter gave him some Fanta. We read a few things to him. Just hanging out together really." Jim looked at us. He was dangerously close to losing his mind. He jumped in the lorry and drove off. We had another smoke with Dave, then the police arrived. A lot of questions were asked. A lot of baffled faces looked at us. We never discovered what really happened to Dave. Like most things in life, he remained a mystery. He did us a favour, because for the next few days Jim left us alone.

Chapter Six: God Gets to Work on Peter

Peter and I were working on a roundabout in Winchmore Hill. We were meant to create a magnificent display of geraniums. We'd been there three hours and smoked a lot of cigarettes and deliberated on God's plan for us. I said I'd take him to a Divine Light Mission meeting. The Old Testament was already colonising his soul, so a bit of variety would help. On the bus that night Peter leaned over to an elderly woman and said: "There is always a sacrifice. Leviticus says: And the skin of the bullock, and all his flesh, with his head, and with his legs, and his inwards, and his dung. And the priest shall take him to a clean place and burn him." To the bus conductor he said "A whale is not a fish."

"What is it then?" Asked the conductor.

"A bird," Peter said with great authority.

At the meeting we listened as a smiling Indian told us that the whole world was an illusion and all that mattered was the Knowledge. Halfway through Peter said he was having an inner vision and he had to cut people down with his tongue.

I followed as he marched to the front and declared very loudly that Guru Maharaj Ji was a false prophet in league with Satan and he, Peter the Rock, was the chosen instrument to renounce him. We were instantly smothered with flowers and white cheesecloth and two divine bouncers got us in enlightened armlocks and bundled us outside. I was kicked down the steps. I asked what had happened to peace and love and a holy smiling Indian bouncer said; "You may say that I'm a dreamer, but I'm not the only one, we hope some day you'll join us, but until then fuck off and learn some manners, cookie boy. Jhaant ke juye."

"Charming. What does Jhaant ke juye mean?"

"Pubic hair lice."

"I bet Gandhi would never say that."

"He would if he'd met you two. Now fuck off. This is a holy place."

We just had time to get a train to Richmond and go to the Buddhist temple to calm ourselves, where a smiling monk told us the world was like cigarette smoke and would disappear into the ether. I told him we'd been assaulted and abused by two holy bouncers and he laughed until he cried. I told him I was going to write to Ravi Shankar and ask him to compose a protest raga about it and the monk laughed so hard he fell over still in the lotus position and we had to untie him from himself.

The next day we sat on the roundabout staring at the wilting geraniums coffined in their boxes. We spent the morning smoking roll ups and discussed the nature of reality. Peter said he had relinquished sex and was going to surrender his sexual energy to God. I asked him how Gail felt about that and he said he hadn't told her yet – he'd only just decided. That night we went to a black revivalist meeting in Tottenham. You could hear them a mile away, whooping and hollering. Peter took to it like a pig to shit. He immediately closed his eyes and started praising the Lord, jigging about like an electrified holy punk. I stood aside a little, half-heartedly muttering nothing in particular. A huge black woman with breasts the size of planets came and crushed me to her vastness.

"Do you feel it? Do you feel it?" She shouted in my ear, rolling her eyes.

"Yes, yes. I feel it, I feel it," I said, panicking as she seemed determined to smother me with faith.

"Where do you feel it?" She bellowed.

"Everywhere."

"Praise the Lord!"

"Praise the Lord!"

"I said – Praise the Lord!"

"And I said – Praise the Lord!"

She dragged me into a circle where everyone hugged and whooped and hollered and praised the Lord.

I staggered out into the cool Tottenham air an hour later with a black eye and two crushed ribs. Peter looked blissful. There was clearly no road he wouldn't travel.

Next morning he had a black eye too. He'd told Gail about becoming celibate and she'd battered him with her clippie's bag which was full of small change and weighed a ton. She'd given him an ultimatum. Her or God. Tough choice, but at least

Gail had the dog's bollocks of tits. God couldn't hope to compete there. Peter still had the problem of Satan following him and took to wearing a handkerchief over his head to stop electrical currents from interfering with his brain and letting the devil in. He was becoming very weird and I thought it was wonderful.

On Friday morning, we sat on the roundabout deciding how to spend the weekend – perhaps a pilgrimage to a cathedral. Perhaps find out where some Jehovah's Witnesses lived and go and harass them or go Quaker hunting. I might become Jewish for the weekend. Life flared with possibilities. The day passed pleasantly enough. The lorry drew up at about 4 pm and Jim the blow up man jumped down. He looked at us aghast. What was his problem? The geraniums were all dried up, still in their trays. The roundabout looked exactly as it had at the beginning of the week. We were both sacked. When we got back to the cabin Dennis intervened and said I could have my job back, but Peter was a no hoper. His career in the parks had lasted exactly one week and he hadn't done a stroke of work the whole time. During the week we'd communed with a dead body, discovered God everywhere, been abused by holy men and smoked a thousand cigarettes. He'd also destroyed his marriage. This was someone I could admire and take seriously. I wouldn't see him for a few months, but when I did life would change forever.

Chapter Seven: Bold Warriors and Kamikaze Parkies

Working for the council meant there was something seriously wrong with you. The nature of your affliction could take many forms; you might be iniquitous, brain damaged, mentally ill, starved of all reason, psychotically paranoid or just plain stupid. When I was moved to Grovelands Park I met a new aspect of deranged council worker – the kamikaze parkie.

Grovelands was a good park. It had class because it had variety. A small wood, open spaces, a 9 hole golf course, a sizable lake where you could row boats and fish all day for two shillings and sixpence and catch gudgeon, tench, and the odd ferocious pike, a putting green, a bird house with peacocks, and trees that sang in the breeze. The council had invented hundreds of arcane rules for the parks that no one ever read and most people didn't even know existed. Except Graham. He'd memorised every syllable and made it his life's work to see they were obeyed to the letter. This meant he spent a lot of his life recovering in hospital. His subliminal death wish was overwhelmingly obvious to everyone except him. He never saw it coming.

He was in his forties, lived with his Mum, had thick pebbley glasses and one roving eye that ticced when he was agitated so when he looked at you it was as if he had a mad little planet in his head dancing in its own swivelling orbit. This eye inflamed many people to violence. He wore the full dark navy park keeper's uniform, including a peaked cap that was too big and kept slipping over his ears, a white shirt and tie and black boots polished to shine like conkers. He dedicated his working life to hunting down transgressors.

He and I were on leaf burning duty. An easy job. You got a lot of leaves and burnt them. We stood watching the smoke and I was humming Rod Stewart's just released Gasoline Alley. Rod had lived near the park before he became famous and little did I know that in a short time I would be in Florida sitting by a pool with the man himself. As the smoke swirled I thought that if a hippy dream of peaceful revolution ever materialised Graham would be miserable because there would be no rules to break and he'd be forced to wear a purple kaftan and butcher striped loons and they would have to tie him down to scrape off his uniform. He'd be so miserable he'd probably kill himself and all because of peaceful revolution. Hippies were dangerous people with their oppressive love and smelly armpits and terrible music. I thought that perhaps hippies really did possess some secret knowledge about life and beauty, but all that most of them possessed were cannabis and head lice. The revolution I was going to start would be more interesting. Something big and bright and dangerously beautiful. Scott Mackenzie would be garrotted. Drugs would be plentiful. The Royal Family would clean toilets. Poetry would be read in the House of Commons. That was as far as I'd got. Details would follow. The angel at my shoulder would steer me ever upstream to where I belonged, or I would die romantically in the attempt at the age of twenty seven. My reverie was broken by a low growling. I thought a mad dog approached, but it was Graham. His revolving eye was hula hooping in his head, magnified by his glasses. His good eye was looking down at the lake. His cheeks plumped with righteousness. A rule was being broken.

Three youths were fishing in the lake. They had cropped hair and stupid faces. All was peaceful. Graham was already striding purposefully towards them, and inevitably to his own doom. I caught up with him.

"Graham. Leave them. They're not doing anything wrong."

"Ha!" he said, as if that explained everything. "Ha!"

He squared up to the three lads and told them the park rules stated quite clearly that fishing had to be pursued at least twelve feet from the boat house and they were no more than ten. They had to move. The three looked at each other and shrugged. They moved their fishing gear a few feet away. This seemed to incense Graham even further. He took a retractable tape measure from his pocket and tested the distance. He then told them they were still six inches too close. The biggest of the three stood and said "Is this a wind up or what?" He was at least a foot taller than Graham, who picked up their fishing gear and threw it in the lake. The youth picked up Graham and threw him in the lake. He came up spluttering and choking and staggered out. He ran at the three youths flailing his fists and shouting that they were barred from the Park, so they picked him up and threw him in the lake again. This happened another three times, at which point Graham was nearly unconscious and the three youths were bored, so they packed up and left. He had swallowed a lot of the lake and had dislocated three fingers as he struggled up the bank.

The next day he was back at work. I tried to stop him from confronting a huge man who was throwing a ball for his dog. He told the man that ball games were not allowed in the park and he confiscated the ball. The man then confiscated Graham's hat and threw it up a tree. He fell as he climbed up to retrieve it and broke his left arm. By Friday he'd had two teeth knocked out by an ex-boxer who had tossed a crust of bread to the ducks after Graham had told him the feeding of wildlife in the parks was expressly forbidden. It was astonishing that he made it to the weekend alive.

The following week I was given a dream of a job. Golf Attendant. I sat in a hut and gave out golf clubs which meant I probably did about five minutes work a day. Less, once I realised that if instead of hosing down the greens, I flooded them so that no one could play until the afternoon when they dried out. It was blissful. I took in my guitar and notebook. I wrote songs and poems. I read Dostoevsky's *The Idiot* and R.D. Laing's *Sanity, Madness and the Family*. I tried to read the *Baghavad Gita* but didn't get far. And I was getting paid. I wanted to know everything. Of course, like all good things, someone had to wreck it.

It was just before 4.30 pm and I was about to close up when two men appeared at the window of my hut. One had a face like a bunch of knuckles.

"Two clubs for nine holes, mate," he said.

I told him the last round was half an hour ago.

"Don't be a prat. Just give us the clubs."

I said I couldn't.

"Just give us the fucking clubs, or I'll come in that shed and break that fucking guitar over your head."

I reconsidered.

“I’m sorry. I didn’t realise you were such keen golfers. My mistake,” I said with a smile and gave him two clubs. He took them without paying. I watched them through the hatch. But now there is someone else. Fuck. Who is it? Of course, it’s Graham, hurtling with surprising speed towards Knucklehead and his accomplice. A serious rule has been broken. Golfing after the allotted time. Nothing can stop him. Graham grabs one of the clubs and tries to pull it away. Knucklehead grabs Graham and throws him to the ground. Graham gets up and charges at him. The club swings around and I hear the sickening kerthump as it beds itself in his head. The men don’t run. Knucklehead calmly finishes his putt, then the two of them slowly walk away. I’m there. Graham has a bruised dent in his forehead, a split where blood and something else oozes out. I know that if he lives he’ll never work in the parks again. And so it was. I got very drunk that night. I left my guitar in the hut and someone stole it. The music was gone from Grovelands. The place seemed to shrink overnight. A shabby bit of green and muddy water in nowhere particular.

Chapter Eight: Mad Monks and the Insanity of Art

All my friends were going mad and I embraced their madness. There was a beauty and poetry in it, before it splintered into mere destruction and harsh angles that lacerated everyone. God was behind a lot of it and I should have started to smell a rat. Instead I launched into everything with a terrifying zest for chaos. A part of me was always invisible, apart, watching and recording, and it was probably this that enabled my survival – the gap at the back of my mind where I could fall when the Reaper came. The goblins didn't see me as the world burnt and shimmered and I was able to escape unseen into my own dreams, where I could hide from them. Of course, I also had the angel at my shoulder watching over me.

Peter telephoned and said he had found God in Sussex, but Satan was hotfoot on his trail. The timing was perfect for me to follow. I had just managed to accidentally burn down the mower shed and cost the Council several thousand pounds. I'd been lucky to escape with my life. I was refuelling the mowers and made the mistake of singing *Sympathy for the Devil* while smoking a cigarette. "Please allow me to introduce myself, I'm a man of wealth and taste..." and on the drawn out last syllable the Benson's fell into the petrol tank of a mower. I escaped with singed eyebrows but the mowers were all fatally wounded and the mower shed was ashes and smoke. Den had no choice but to sack me. He said all I had to do was reapply for work in Parks and Recreation in a few months time and I'd get my job back. The Council never refuses the incompetent, the stupid, and the insane for long.

So it was I arrived at a monastery in Haywards Heath. Peace, prayer and holiness. Or so I thought. It turned out to be more mayhem and madness and destruction. There were two monks, four novitiates and about six outcasts like me in search of enlightenment. Also a little man called Michael who was dying of cancer but ate enough for six horses every day. It seemed that the more the cancer consumed him the more he ate, perhaps as a way of keeping death at bay.

Anchorhold had a small stipend from the church, so there was a pottery and a huge loom that filled a whole room, to make things to sell. Head monk was Father Slade, a Cowley Father with a gift for taking the heat out of my brain at bad moments when the universe seemed about to explode, and which he achieved by placing his hands at the back of my head and rubbing fiercely. Small electric shocks sparked and shot around the room, then I felt quiet and able to cope with simple tasks, like breathing and making tea. He was small, white haired, had been to India as a missionary, but came back as everything. He liked to garden but could never cut anything down. He took a saw to a tree once and said it started screaming. A squirrel fell in love with him and lived in the pockets of his monk's habit. Instinctively knowing when Father Slade was bored with someone, the squirrel would come out, run all over his head and down into the other pocket. This effectively shut up people. Anchorhold was a Benedictine monastery but infused too with all things Eastern, tai-chi, and anything else he found of use, ideal for someone of my eclectic tastes. His number two was Brother Gerald, a nearly blind albino who was in charge of the loom. Some of us saw this as a drawback, as Brother Gerald could barely find his way into the room, let alone work the loom. It led to very little actually being made, nothing at all sold, but a lot of interesting accidents. Once, Brother Gerald got a thread from his robe caught in the loom and wove himself into a cocoon, so that he looked like a large white headed mummified moth in battered underpants and we had to cut him free with pinking shears. Another time, peering and squinting too closely, he wove his own hair into a cushion cover and we had to shave half his head to free him.

One of the novitiates was Roger, a complete arsehole. He tried to look holy by smiling and looking slightly above your head when he spoke, as if moved by some distant vision, and he wrote pretentiously crap poems about orange flowers and girls' bottoms. I prayed fervently that he'd fall into a combine harvester, which is not very Christian, but I just couldn't see a place for a nobhead like Roger in the revolutionary paradise on earth I was busy imagining. There would be saints, mad prophets, vestal virgins and big hearted whores, leaders and followers, gypsies of the soul, drug ruined musicians, Peter Green would find his sanity again, mischievous sprites, jugglers and clowns, all manner of souls, but Fuckface Roger would not be invited. Peter and I made it our solemn religious duty to make his life as much of a misery as was divinely possible. We mocked the piety of his prayers, the warbling of his singing during matins, the sanctimonious manner in which he delivered his god awful poems. I wrote a parody of one of them:

Crap Poem Number 657 by Roger the Dipshit

You dress in silk
I bring you orange flowers
And this poem
Which you say is
The biggest crock of buffalo shit
You've ever heard
And tell me to
Shove the flowers up my
Fat ginger arse.

I sent it to Roger as a Christmas present but he never replied. Some people fail to see when you are trying to help them.

Peter was becoming seriously strange, but I listened as he told me there was a great war coming in which Satan would constantly appear as a false prophet and we should be on the lookout for him. We saw him everywhere in the faces of bus conductors, butchers, hairdressers and policeman – it was a full time job. It was like being a bona fide vampire hunter. Peter was also worried about the nuns in the convent next door. We went to the funeral of one of the elderly nuns and Peter was convinced that when darkness fell, a few of the sisters turned into giant crows and pecked at his dreams. He was starting to identify with Job. He would go up to strangers in the street, including little old ladies, and say "Gird up now thy loins like a man; for I will demand of thee, and answer thou me." He cornered the postman in the pottery room and said "My breath is corrupt, my days are extinct, the graves are ready for me. Are there not mockers with me?...Should a wise man utter vain knowledge, and fill his belly with the east wind?...Canst thou bind the unicorn with his band in the furrow?"

The postie backed into a corner, petrified and dropping letters like confetti. Peter pursued him, shouting now: "I have sewed sackcloth upon my skin, and defiled my horn in the dust…all my members are as a shadow…I have said to corruption, Thou art my father: to the worm, Thou art my mother, and my sister." The postie smashed open the back door and escaped. The Old Testament is a barrel of serpents once you dive in. Complaints were received so we then had to collect our own post, but Father Slade was a trooper of the spirit, unfazed by the hysterics of the unenlightened. Peter closed his eyes and fled into silence when the screaming panics really got their barbs in him. His ex-wife Gail came to visit him and afterwards, Father Slade said that given the size of her breasts, it was no wonder Peter had become so unstable. By now I realised he was going somewhere alone, or perhaps I was too much of a coward to follow. He wanted to disappear into a mystery; perhaps something was compelling him into one. There was a light in him but he was fatally entranced with the darkness waiting for us all who really wanted to push the boat out into the great unknown, ourselves on it.

I'm fast asleep in the dark and a voice hisses in my ear, "I've committed apostasy." I bang my head on the light above the bed as I wake up expecting a lunatic has got in. I'm right. It's Peter, his eyes like fluorescent elliptical mirrors in the moonlight. I see my fading terror reflect back in them.

"I'm an apostate," he says. "Swords keep coming into my mind."

"Throw them out," I suggest. He ignores this.

"When they come to arrest Christ, what does Peter do? He smites the high priest's servant, Malchus, and cuts off his right ear. What does that mean?"

"It means he's only got one ear," I say.

"It means the disciples carried weapons. Jesus said: 'Do not think that I came to bring peace on the earth; I did not come to bring peace, but a sword. For I came to set a man against his father, and a daughter against her mother, and a daughter-in-law against her mother-in-law; and a man's enemies will be the members of his household.' Are you thinking what I'm thinking?"

"No," I said, then a moment later, "What are you thinking?"

"That we ought to arm ourselves. Against our own families. Against Armageddon."

"Then I'm definitely not thinking what you are. Go to bed, Peter."

"Satan said, "'My name is legion. For we are many.'"

"Not to me he didn't."

"What did he say to you?"

"My name is Nick, for I am a policeman."

"God likes a sense of humour."

"Then we have something in common at last. Go to bed, Peter."

"I have to purify myself." He was gone. Next morning his room was empty, except for a razorblade and a page torn from the Bible. The beginning of the Gospel of St. John. I didn't see Peter for months.

Given the oddness of the people at Anchorhold, it was just like working for the Council, only accompanied by prayer and meditation rather than flatulence and obscenities. One of the people there was Mario, a hook nosed, raven haired artist recovering from a nervous breakdown. Intense, brooding, and a painter of chaotic messes that looked like donkey vomit, but with titles like "Christ in Paradise", "Vision of Gethsemane", "Triumph of Resurrection." His wife, an exhausted looking woman with skin frail as butterfly wings, visited him occasionally and Mario would go into full dramatic mode: sighs, great meaningless sweeping gestures of his hands, the odd tear. Apart from creating bilious messes on canvas, he lay on his bed and did fuck all. Sometimes he didn't even bother to get up.

One day he asked me into his room and told me that long ago a woman had given him an erection nine inches long. I congratulated him. He asked what the biggest erection I'd ever had was. About three feet, I said, but at the time I did have my willy stuck in a lead pipe and was trying to pull it out. He didn't laugh. He said he wanted to do a few figurative paintings and asked if I'd model for him. Five minutes later I was bollock naked and standing like a Greek athlete, in stance if not physique. Mario sat on the bed scrutinising my cock and making furious little flicks with his paint brush. Monastic life was proving to be very odd. The painting he did looked like a cross between emu and a garden rake with a drug problem.

That evening at supper Mario wasn't there. He'd probably gone to bed to have another breakdown. Father Slade asked if everyone had had a rewarding day. I should have kept my mouth shut but the angel at my shoulder whispered "Go on. Do it," so I told them Mario had asked me to strip naked and spent a lot of time looking at my todger and did a lousy painting. Brother Gerald choked on an olive and wiped his glasses furiously for the next five minutes. Father Slade coughed politely and said Grace. The next day there was a lot of shouting in Mario's room and shortly afterwards he was out mowing the lawn – the peacefulness of his breakdown was over and now he'd have to work for his dinner. I felt a bit guilty but what the hell – it was interesting to make things happen, and anyway it was the angel at my shoulder who had prompted me. I could tell the way Mario was forcing the mower too quickly, and shuffling too close, that disaster was a moment away. Before lunchtime he'd cut off a toe. Afterwards he kept to his room and took up landscape painting. I decided it was not God's plan for me to be a monk. I had divine and revolutionary business in the world beyond. And at some point, I had to go to university to become a clever bastard. For now, my job back at Parks and Recreation would do.

Chapter Nine: An Accidental Marriage, a Drastic Haircut and a Dream about God

I suddenly got married by accident. It was a complete disaster – a pattern I was to repeat unfailingly throughout my life. I blame the Old Testament and God. Her name was Jess and I gave her a lift home from a party on my Vespa scooter. I had to keep stopping to be sick in people's front gardens. It had been a long night, ending at six am with Jess and I snogging fiercely and her daring me to run naked around the block. I had felt her breasts during the whole of *Dark Side of the Moon* and another crazy from the Council, John Basham, was asleep across us, a tomato sandwich on his head and snoring loudly. Jess had a voice that made me think she might lick warm honey off my body.

In between marathon snogs and while holding on firmly to one of her breasts, I started to drunkenly intone Solomon's Song, which is one of the sexiest and strangest love poems ever written. "Thy hair is a flock of goats that appear from Gilead. Thy teeth are as a flock of sheep which go up from the washing, whereof every one beareth twins, and there is not one barren among them. As a piece of pomegranate are thy temples within thy locks…Thy two breasts are like two young roes that are twins…thine eyes like the fishpools in Heshbon, by the gate of Bathrabbim: thy nose is as the tower of Lebanon which looketh towards Damascus." Something in it entranced her, the undulating rhythms and exotic images, or perhaps it was the cider and pills she'd been swallowing all night. John Basham woke up and was looking at me, astonished. "You bastard," he said, "You tell a bird she's got hair like a goat's, teeth like a flock of fucking sheep, nose like a tower block, a head like a bit of fruit and tits and eyes like a fish, and she practically puts out for you on the sofa. What's your fucking trick?"

"It's the Holy Spirit moving through me, and the angel at my shoulder," I told him.

"Spirit my dick; angel my arse," he said, and fell asleep on my hot aching crotch.

Conquered by the Old Testament Jess said if I'd run naked around the block she'd marry me and, stupidly, it seemed a good idea at the time. We were on a council estate in Edmonton and I figured nobody would be around except milkmen and a few red eyed insomniacs, maybe the odd murderer coming home. If I really pounded the pavement it would take less than ten minutes. Off came my kit and I was out into a cold dawn, a gallon of cider, a few joints and a few yellow pills I'd taken accidentally swilling around inside me, the memory of Jess's breasts still warming my fingertips.

All went well until I was on the home stretch. A man was coming towards me, his little collie dog on a lead. The dog looked familiar. It was Diana, my Uncle Herbert's dog. Which meant there was a very good chance the man was my uncle Herbert. Which it was. I decided not to break step and keep jogging. As we passed he said "Morning Steve. " "Morning Uncle Bert." He never invited me to go horse riding with his daughter Janice again. I think he feared for the horse.

I knew it was a mistake to get married but somehow it just happened. Some things take you by surprise. Even more surprised was a lovely girl called Sue whom I was seeing. It came as a bit of a shock when I said I couldn't see her the coming weekend because I was getting married. It was a time of generous confusion and we stayed friends. She even said she'd come to the wedding if she had nothing better to do.

It was a church wedding with a priest and flowers and tears, presents and a sense of imminent doom. Apart my immediate family I didn't know most of the people there; even the bride was a stranger. Then some of the lads from Parks and Recreation came. Mick the Dick tried to seduce Jess immediately after the ceremony by getting in the car with her and slamming the door on me. He was arrested later for flashing at two of the bridesmaids. Terry started a fight with the bride's mother and the police had to be called. Two lads called Dog and Boss stole the piano from the hall where we had the reception; it was extraordinary that no one saw them. Two druggies I knew, John Spicer and Pat Duggan, brought some really strong hash brownies and after downing three of them, my Auntie Lil had a psychotic breakdown and my Uncle Frank had to be coaxed down from the roof after thinking he was a starling called Paris. Dennis got drunk and sobbed on my dad's shoulder while Julie tried to entice me to go in the cloakroom with her, to discuss our friendship, she said, with her knee wedged between my legs and working my crotch with all the dexterity of a squirrel fondling a beloved nut. Lucky the dog was there, his leg in a splint and tail three inches shorter. I had my head shaved as a mild protest and looked like a mad boiled egg. I tried to explain to everyone before the ceremony that this was all a horrible mistake. "Nerves," said my Aunt Peg. "have a good upchuck in the men's and you'll be all right." The only person who listened was my Gran. "It's all a mistake," I said to her. "Course it is. All marriages are mistakes. Intimate relationships are horrible things. Unnatural. Run now while you got a chance," she said helpfully. I didn't run.

After a night of frenzied drinking I drove us down in my clapped out mini to Porlock for a honeymoon in the Lorna Doone hotel. I had the mother of all hangovers and took a fistful of amphetamines in the foolish hope it would stabilise me. I gibbered complete twaddle for three hours, then the exhaust fell off, and in the erroneous belief I was a mechanic I got under the car, unscrewed the petrol valve and got covered in petrol. My skin came off like a giant pink glove and I spent the first night of marriage covered in calamine lotion and reading Sartre's *Roads to Freedom*. The angel at my shoulder had never laughed so much. We spent a week going for walks, calamining my burnt body, my taking a lot of speed, and I meditated daily whilst doing a headstand against the wall as I'd been told it raised your consciousness. At end of the week I was burnt inside and out and decided not to take speed or cover myself in petrol again. There were plenty of other drugs and experiences that might lead to enlightenment. Jess went off over the blue horizon to make a mess of her life and I went in the opposite direction to do the same with mine. Our marriage lasted seven and a half days. I kept a marble casserole dish and she took everything else. I was hungry for the open spaces of the parks, and thirsty for new knowledge.

On the night we parted I had a dream that made me think angels were more complicated than I'd imagined:

God shifted on his throne. His arse ached. Too much sitting around. Haemorrhoids. Jesus, it's so undignified, he thought, shifting his weight to the other divine haunch and thinking of Preparation H. Somewhere near or far cherubs and seraphims were warming up for a night of singing. Gabriel stood before him, his huge wings ruffling in the breeze, his finely honed torso glistening gold in the heavenly light, his perfectly chiselled features giving nothing away. Not a hair out of place. Arrogant bastard, thought God. Why do I never know what he's thinking? I'm meant to be omniscient, so why is this narcissus a foreigner to me?

"So," God began, "what's all this I've been hearing about you?"

"I don't know," said Gabriel, with a slight sneer. "If you're the one who's hearing things, perhaps you should be telling me."

Time was, angels knew their place, God thought wearily. Time was, they'd all crap themselves when I called them in. Everything was changing, getting stale. No respect these days.

"What I hear, Gabriel, is that you're thinking of joining the other side."

"You mean Lucifer?"

"Don't say his name up here!" Screamed God, as clouds exploded, his throne rattled, cherubs wet their pants and rainbows drained of colour.

"What – Lucifer?" Said Gabriel. Three angels had massive coronaries. God's haemorrhoids screamed. "As a matter of fact, he's been headhunting me for months. I've been made an offer."

"What could he possibly offer you that I can't?" Boomed God.

"Permission to dally with earthly virgins. And I get to dream up new things for hell. I was thinking of a head shredder for impure thoughts and a tongue brace for blasphemers. A new form of leprosy that turns people into crocodiles, the first born of every family to have two extra mouths instead of eyes..."

As Gabriel went on God suddenly felt tired. And very old. This endless violence and suffering. Retribution and punishment. Hatred and pain. From where did it all emanate? From Him, of course. What had he been thinking of? It was all so unrelenting. He needed something new. Something different. A gimmick. Someone to take over at least some of the responsibility. A son maybe?

"Gabriel," he said. "How would you like to father a child for me?"

Gabriel looked interested.

Then it stopped. This dream was trying to tell me something. I didn't have a clue what it was.

Chapter Ten: Drugs and Death and Disasters

If you wait long enough everything goes wrong. You just have to be patient. Enlightenment still seemed a long way off and university even further. My world revolution was all coming together in my head, but nowhere else. I started spending a lot of time with a few demented drug users. They both worked in Parks and Recreation, so there was ample time for serious abuse.

In the late 60s and early 70s there were a lot of suburban drug houses. The house fronts looked respectable, but in many roads, cushioned between upright families with decent jobs and aspirations, would be a temple of narcotics and jasmine inhabited by brightly plumed young wastrels who talked a lot about karma and star signs and things being far out, whilst rearranging their brains and pummelling internal organs into submission. In the morphology of hippiedom the people in these drug temple suburbias were revolutionary agnostics, more interested in Bacchanalian and Dionysian excess than spiritual deliverance. I floated in and out of their circles. I liked the drugs, and listening to Hendrix, the Incredible String Band and Hawkwind, but got bored sitting cross-legged all night in a circle on a cheap Indian rug waiting for the joint to come round, then waiting to see who would enter a coma first. Conversation was pretty limited. If you could say "Wow" and "Far out" then you'd get by for several years.

John Spicer lived in one of these houses. He and Pat Duggan worked with me. Their attitude was that it was cool to sit under a tree taking mescalin or smoking strong hash all day and get paid for it by the Council, then go home and use your wages to buy more drugs and sit on a filthy rug taking them until you fell over. Arguably, the Council's Department of Parks and Recreation financed more drug taking than any Moroccan or South American cartel. John was a Pantheist, believing that God and the universe are one. His intellectual justification for this was along the lines of "Y'know, it's like all one. Just. I mean, y'know, like everything is everything else. It's just, y'know, like all one." In more lucid moments he had an annoying habit of trying to speak in old English, "My needments are few"; "Come hither with thine stash bag, good fellow." Long wispy brown hair hung down to his waist, a fu Manchu moustache hid his lips and he was even thinner than me. He wore crushed velvet loons and his girlfriend's Indian silk top. It was rumoured he washed on his birthday.

Pat was thinner than both of us, only ever wore black, had a mass of frizzy hair and the worst skin I've ever seen, a rippled landscape of spots and craters and uninvited plooks and rosacea. I imagined his soul as a pale cyst. He was a drug dealer who still lived in his parents' council house. His dreams were fugitive and despairing. He said that if only he had a talent for something he'd be ambitious, but he didn't, so what was the point in bothering? It didn't occur to him that you might have to put in a bit of effort to achieve something, but I suppose his personal nihilism gave him tragic status, in his own mind at least. We are authors of our own ills and triple calamity was about to flip over our lives. After a hard day at work, sitting under a beech tree meditating and smoking grass, we went to Spicer's house of hash for an evening session.

Others were there. Two lads and three girls. Girls could always tell how well endowed a guy was because the loons were so punishingly tight around the crotch you could see the exact shape and size, and your voice went up an octave, whereas it was more difficult to gauge a girl's figure, as so many wore, like Leonard Cohen's Suzanne, rags and feathers from Salvation Army counters. Also, they had so much kohl around their eyes, it was sometimes disconcertingly like kissing a badger. One of the girls, Lin Robinson, was out of place with her plump apple cheeks, bright dark eyes and rude good health. We played the Incredible String Band song, *Air*, over and over again until even the record player was bored, then we played Steppenwolf's *Born to be Wild.* John had taken some mescaline and something new he'd been given from a mate just back from Afghanistan. It was a large brown pill and could have easily been a dried goat turd as a mind altering chemical. After an hour or so he disappeared. An hour after that, but it may have been six, I went to look for him. He was on his bed, pale and inert. He was usually pale and inert, in fact so cadaverous it was sometimes difficult to know if he was still alive, so it didn't register at first, until I noticed the white foam on his moustache. I thought he'd been at the whipped cream or had a snotty sneeze in his sleep or indulged some odd sexual perversion, but it was too milky and viscous, and a thin sheen of sweat covered his whole face.

I called out his name. I tried to shake him awake. I slapped his face. Nothing. I listened to his chest. I couldn't tell if it was a heart beat or Steppenwolf blasting through the ceiling. I went down to Pat.

"John's either dead or in a coma."

Pat looked at me vacantly.

"I said John's in a coma. Or dead."

"Cool," said Pat, and suddenly lay back as if shot in the head and started snoring. At least he wasn't dead. All the others were passed out. Lin Robinson had gone home to bake pies or bottle plums or something. Fifteen minutes later the ambulance arrived. The crew looked around the place in disgust. I hadn't really noticed that, apart from unconscious bodies, the living room was full of strange gases and takeaway Chinese meals in various stages of decomposition, and a lot of cat poo. An alabaster statue of the Buddha wore eye make up and had a long joint stuck in the mouth; a garish wooden carving of the goddess Kali had a condom stretched over her head and a few mouldy carrots stuck under her many armpits. John was seriously unconscious as they stretchered him out. I accompanied him to hospital; the doctor said his heart had stopped several times and that technically, he'd died at least twice. I thought this mighty impressive and wondered what stories he'd have to tell – lights at end of tunnels, whole life flashing past and plash of the ferryman's oars. Perhaps he'd chatted to the Reaper or had a flash of God himself. In fact he had nothing to say about it. He remembered zilch about death but developed a passion for binding things up with duct tape and for creating small explosions.

A few weeks later I went with Pat to his house at lunchtime to borrow some records. I'd accrued a huge collection of borrowed records and such was the generosity of the time that no one thought it cool to ask for them back. We were in his tiny bedroom with Hendrix's *Band of Gypsys* playing ridiculously loud. Even before anything happened I was uncomfortable because the album cover was the old 'unlucky' one with the models of Hendrix, Brian Jones, John Peel and Bob Dylan. The first two had already gone with the Reaper and, presumably, no one wanted to tempt fate, and the doomed cover was withdrawn, or so the apocryphal story went. It seemed ominous just looking at it. Suddenly the door burst open and Pat's Dad stood there, angry beyond reason. He looked at us with contempt. I could see why he was disappointed in Pat, who was Oxfam thin, wasted, uncommunicative, and whose only ambition was to be in a coma. His Dad was shouting but the music was so loud we couldn't hear him.

"Bloody row!" He snapped off the record player. Just looking at us seemed to annoy him even more. "Look at you. Bloody useless. He can get out. Go on, get out of my house!" This was me.

"He's my friend," said Pat.

"Get out!" His Dad shouted at my face.

"It's fine. I'm going," I said, grabbing an armful of albums, but not the doomed, cursed *Band of Gypsys.* I went downstairs, Pat following. His Dad then made the fatal mistake of pushing Pat down the last few stairs.

"Don't push me!" Pat said, turning on him.

"Go on, you can get out too!" His Dad shouted. He pushed Pat, who pushed back. There was hatred and violence in the air. It had obviously been there for years and was now a boil being lanced. They looked like machines about to break apart on each other. Suddenly his Dad was down, purple faced, holding his chest and gasping for breath. His Mum came from the kitchen and looked in horror at her husband fighting to get air inside him. Pat looked up at me, paler than ever, and hissed "Go!" I opened the front door and went to the gate. A few minutes later Pat came out with a huge plastic bag bursting with amphetamines, uppers, downers and hash.

"I think I killed my dad. This is my stash. Look after it. The police are coming." He went back inside. I hid the stash under a little concrete bridge over Salmon's Brook, where John Keats used to walk to Enfield Town from his apothecary's shop in Edmonton. I thought of Pat's Dad's mouth turning purple, as if some terrible internal bruising was taking place. The lines "beaded bubbles winking at the brim, And purple-stained mouth" came to mind. His Dad would be fine. These were the years of love and peace and reconciliation. He'd be fine. But, perversely, he was dead by the time the ambulance crew and police arrived.

I didn't see Pat for a few weeks. He never came back to work. Then I saw him as I passed his house and caught up with him. I told him where his stash was but he didn't seem interested. "I'm really sorry about your Dad," I said. He looked at me, expressionless. "It's alright. We didn't get on." That was it. We went for a pint and he didn't mention his father again. Even though I still couldn't pronounce his name, I'd started to read some Nietzsche in anticipation of being a clever bastard at University and thought "He who fights monsters should see to it he himself does not become a monster, for if you stare at the abyss, the abyss stares back at you." Some people fall into the abyss. Some people push themselves into it. I was starting to think that thought itself was a kind of faith, but one in which you took responsibility for yourself rather than heaping it all onto an external god. Perhaps our gods were becoming internal and we made offerings to them in the form of drugs and drink and self destruction in the vain hope they would not be too antagonistic and punitive towards us. Pat's gods seemed to have withered on the skinny vine.

Three months pass. I am at the Cooks Ferry Inn in North London; it is small and either intolerably sweaty or arctic cold, but you can be up close to many of the best bands and musicians: Spencer Davis Group, Mott the Hoople, Led Zeppelin, Clapton, Jeff Beck, Rod Stewart, Ron Wood, the Who, Graham Bond, Alexis Korner, the wonderful Peter Green. Many of the best English blues guitarists ever cut their teeth here, usually apprenticing in John Mayall's Bluesbreakers. It is a Monday. Graham Bond is just finishing an alto sax solo that soars from despair to the most sublime madness, as Bond himself does, and I wonder if music is better than sex and poetry and god, when I see Pat by the door. He's thinner and paler, as if he is disappearing. He doesn't see me. I follow him outside, just to say Hi. He goes down to the car park and gets in a mini with another guy, who is driving. I see the whole thing slowly. The car park at the Ferry Inn is at the back and you have to drive out at an angle, up a steepish short slope on a bend to the road. I don't know if the driver is stoned, drunk, demented, bad, or just unlucky, perhaps all of those, but the car misses a gear and rolls back down the slope. I see Pat's face as a white blob in the great dark, just before the mini upends with a surprisingly quiet galoop into the dark canal.

A swish as the car sinks almost immediately and a curtain of water billows over and back, like an indifferent caress, and two white faces with barely time to understand that this really is it. No more no mores. Help came too late. The Ferryman was there before the ambulance and police. I don't know if he made them pay or thought the drowning itself was payment enough. Pat's star was doomed to crash and he seemed burdened by the weight of his own life on those skinny hooped shoulders. Life swallowed him just as the water did.

A few years later on 8th May 1974 Graham Bond jumped under a train at Finsbury Park Tube Station. I was very sorry because I think he should have chosen Mornington Crescent or Green Park, even Camden Town would have been classier. It's not the Piccadilly line I am against; it's the god awful station. Finsbury Park was and is a dump of a place, though it did have great concerts at the Astoria and is near the Arsenal ground, and Steve Marriott's Packet of Three band played in local pubs for a few quid. Bond wasn't good looking or glamorous, he was fat and had a raspy growling blues voice, not the stuff of stardom in pop music. He had a serious drug and drink problem, flirted with dangerous dark magic and came to believe he was the son of Alistair Crowley. I still don't think they are good enough excuses for choosing Finsbury Park to top yourself. His alto sax solo lived on and I could hear it echoing across the canal where I often sat, hungover, trying to remember what the hell I had been up to the night before. I don't think Pat's already funereal life was really mourned at all, except for the ghost of Bond's music that covered the water and soared and cried and whispered for all those who lose and fail. Which is all of us finally.

Chapter Eleven: Revenge is a Dish Best Served with Relish

It is good to play God. Everyone should do it at least once. Their names were Harry and Eddie and some spider monkey in the council had put them together in a park in Palmers Green so that Harry could torture Eddie. They were Jekyll and Hyde, Cain and Abel, Chalk and Cheese, Tom and Jerry. In the little hut they inhabited, there was violence and rebuke in the air, misery in the biscuit tin, despair in the teabags.

It was worse. Someone, in a fit of bureaucratic and homicidal stupidity and with the Council's obsession with hierarchies, made Harry supervisor. Who was there to supervise? Only Eddie. Harry took his new responsibility seriously. He made Eddie do everything: the mowing, weeding, sweeping, trimming, digging, watering the flowers, opening and locking up, tea making, cleaning the toilet which Harry ensured was always in a disgusting state with all manner of things thrown down the bowl which Eddie had to fish out. He once had to dislodge a pork pie and a balaclava with his bare hands from the u bend.

Harry gave despots a bad name. Eddie was his nation, his slave army, one which he abused on a daily basis. The whole working day was a filigree of small humiliations, chastisements, tortures and evil put downs. The sole purpose of Harry's life was to make Eddie's a misery and the sole purpose of Eddie's was to endure it. I was tossed into this empire of abuse and desolation for a week, to help plant out some shrubs. It was painful to see. Here was Stalin, Idi Amin, Vlad the Impaler, Darth Vader and Nobby Nelson, my old psychotic people-hating woodwork teacher, all rolled in one. I vowed that one day Harry and all the repressive forces he represented would be swept into ignominy and the outer reaches of hell once the new world I was busy imagining transpired. I would give Eddie his own Kew Gardens when my beautiful revolution came to pass, transforming England into the New Jerusalem, darkness into starlight, hopelessness into heaven. I was Che Guevara of the soul. All this would surely happen. How and when was another matter, but happen it would. I could start small. Here. Now.

And what did Harry do all day, apart from torture Eddie? Mornings were spent dozing, reading the *Sun* as if it was *War and Peace*, swilling tea, smoking Number Six and putting things down the toilet for Eddie to fish out. Afternoons were spent on cars. He fancied himself a mechanic, although the internal combustion engine was a foreign country to him. Nevertheless there seemed to be no shortage of imbeciles for him to fleece, mugs who would foolishly drive their cars into the park, then pay him to systematically destroy whatever parts were still working. As Einstein said, the only two infinites are space and human stupidity. I should know, I was one of the mugs. Harry transformed my battered but functioning mini into a large oil leak on wheels and charged me fifteen quid. He smirked as he pocketed the notes and I pushed the car from the park to the knackers' yard. Enough was enough. Righteous justice was imminent. Call out the instigators, because there's revolution in the air.

I tried to give Eddie some visionary comfort.

"I weave a golden thread around you," I said, circling my hands slowly around his head. "You are the godhead, safe in the cradle of your own divinity. The rustlings of leaves are heavenly choirs praising you, the flowers a gilded carpet to put wings on your ankles, ladybirds are spotted warrior angels protecting you, when you mow the grass you are Phaethon in his golden chariot. Your life is a continuous melody playing out to infinity. You are immortal, Eddie."

He sneezed and hawked up a great gobbet of mucous, like the diseased lung of a dead fairy. "Bloody hayfever," he said snottily. I tried to inspire him with the poetry of rebuke:

"I curse thee! Let a sufferer's curse
Clasp thee, his torturer, like remorse,
Till thine infinity shall be
A robe of envenomed agony;
And thine omnipotence a crown of pain,
To cling like burning gold round thy dissolving brain."

Eddie sort of got it, but not quite. He just smiled wistfully and said "I like the bit about his brain dissolving." The council was not, it must be said, a hotbed of poetry appreciation. Action was required, and who was to be the deliverer? Me. Angel of Retribution. Eddie's pleasure in the dissolving brain gave me an idea.

John Spicer had sold me some of the strongest hash I'd ever smoked. One blow and madness beckoned. Great spaces opened up in your head and your legs twitched uncontrollably. The world became a vast stage set with moving interconnected parts that took your breath away. You tried to eat everything, including yourself. You would gladly auction your heart to cannibals. You entered cities of ferocious kissing. It primed and heated all internal organs. It gave me an instant erection that could only be cooled with a sock full of ice cubes. Brilliant stuff. Nectar for the gods. I bought enough to fell a large herd of bison. Harry was going to get the lot, all in one go. Then we'd see some r and r.

I waited for an auspicious moment. It came. It was Eddie's birthday. We sat in the tiny tea room, Harry reading the Sun, Eddie looking at his one birthday card which I'd given him. I asked Harry if he'd join us at the pub lunchtime to have a birthday drink for Eddie. His ratty eyes appeared over the paper. They were red and inflamed because it was 17 November 1970 and today was the appearance of the first topless Page Three girl, Stefanie Rahn, and Harry had been looking at her tits for about two hours solid.

"Who's buying?" He asked suspiciously.

"Me," I said.

"Sandwiches?"

"Even better. Cake."

At eleven thirty I brought out a small chocolate cake. Harry loved it. We generously let him scoff the lot. I didn't tell him there was enough hash in it to send up an air balloon. By twelve we were in the pub. Harry's eyes were the size of saucers. He stared into his pint as if Jesus Christ's head was about to pop out. I clapped my hands and Harry fell off his chair as if the world had exploded. We helped him back up. Veils of habit were being replaced by delirium and feverish dreams. Harry would never be the same – he had already roasted enough brain cells to dine in outer space for years. Whether it left him a better human being with compassion, or a drooling cretin, was, as yet, unknown, but even the latter would be a monster improvement on the old Harry. He sat smiling seductively at Guz the grizzled barman, who had a face like a stocking full of walnuts. Guz was tolerant of hippies and druggies and loved rock and roll but he hated "pant stabbing homos." If this continued Guz would take him out the back and nut him into next week.

"Happy Birthday, Eddie," I said, raising my glass. "I'm sure Harry would like to do a little party piece in honour of the occasion." I moved until I swam into Harry's misty focus. "How about you take off your trousers, stand on the table and sing *My Boy Lollipop* to Eddie?"

Like an automaton Harry stood up and unbuckled his trousers, then got on the table and started singing. He looked repulsive. Grey stained old y-fronts that had probably been a dishcloth in World War II, and little knobbly knees. He really went for the song, smiling like a perverted elf: "My boy lollipop, you make my heart go giddyup, you set my heart on fiyah, you are my one desiyah…" Tears of joy streamed down Eddie's face. Aeons of humiliation and misery were dissolving and he started to look years younger. Revenge is a beautiful thing, as I'd learnt from the Old Testament, and, as the man said, is a dish best served cold. I'd brought my instamatic and got a good six shots before Guz grabbed Harry, opened the door, and threw him out into the street amid cheers and applause. I bought another pint for Eddie to celebrate not just his birthday but a major blow for the revolution and a redressing of balance in the universe.

We left the pub just in time to see Harry being arrested for molesting a lamppost whilst in possession of an elephantine erection. The police eventually let him off with a warning, but he got a severe reprimand from the Council, a letter that went on for twelve pages saying that he had brought the reputation of Parks and Recreation into severe disrepute and had violated the following codes of conduct: items 36 A, F, G and H, items 243B, C and D, sub clause 29, para. 4B, and addendum 16 D. It didn't come sterner than that. They demoted him. Plus, Eddie had the gloriously incriminating photographs to produce every time

Harry tried to chuck his weight about. No more pork pies and balaclavas down the toilet. A little kingdom had its equanimity restored. A wrong had been righted. The vengeance of the Lord had been visited upon Harry. I thought the angel at my shoulder should be pleased.

Brian Jones – A doomed mischief-hunting pixie who could pick up any instrument and make it sing.

A typical Parks and Recreation worker from the 1970s.

Paul Kossoff – the doomed virtuoso guitarist of Free.

Guru Maharaj Ji – a mutated Roy Orbison on the make.

I'm the shaggy haired one, the other is a rock god.

Tiny Tim. Photo: pinterest.com/boxmonkeymusic

Alexis Korner. Photo: Heinrich_Klaffs_Collection_99

Chapter Twelve: The Mad Mystic and the Resurrection of the Leg

I had been given the job of scraping out the bottom of a paddling pool in Oakwood Park, then scrubbing it with an industrial broom. It was full of duck shit, swan shit, pigeon shit and now dog shit. Probably some alien shit in there too. It was a shit job and no two ways.

A new guy was with me. Henry. He'd started that morning and hadn't said a word yet. He was about forty, with sparse scraps of wiry hair as if he'd pulled out great lumps in exasperation, a wounded smile and feverish eyes. I looked at the crap daggled gunge at the bottom of the pool and decided to have a Benson's before actually doing anything. The new guy clearly liked the idea of having a break before work and sat next to me. I had a lot on my mind. Chaos, death, god, the gorgeous revolution I was going to spearhead, the breath-taking tits of a girl called Annie that bobbed like divine apples beneath a low cut cheesecloth shirt. I had no money – no one I knew did, but we barely thought about it. Our aspirations were to alter our brains, hurl ourselves into the mystery of the universe, and change the world. I don't think I ever had a long conversation about money until years later, when it suddenly seemed to matter to everyone. Money was irrelevant to the song we were singing. Whenever it was mentioned Peter would say "Give Caesar what is due to Caesar," and that was enough.

The silence didn't bother me. I liked it and lay back to look at clouds and smoke a few more Bensons. Conversations are sometimes an intrusion. The presence of other people diminishes me in the company of clouds. I wondered why some were lower than others. My mind seemed a sky through which clouds travel. They were eclipsed by a large smiling head. The new guy was leaning over and looking at me. He'd decided it was time to make contact.

"All created is most of sensitive sorrow the things."

What the fuck? Another nutter. He said it again and smiled. I smiled back. Fucking Professor Stanley Unwin to spend all day with.

"Is one long moment suffering very," he said.

I looked at him and wished he was a cloud. He tapped his head with both fists theatrically, as if realising he hadn't explained properly.

"Alphabetically I only speak," he said smiling more broadly. I understood. He only spoke alphabetically and would rearrange the words of a sentence in alphabetical order, based on the first letter of the word, before he uttered them. This was mental but interesting. I translated his first two remarks. "Sorrow is the most sensitive of all created things" and "Suffering is one very long moment." Wordsworth. Wonderful. Suddenly the day opened up with ripe possibilities. I asked him why he did it. He said it was to "devil listening stop the" (stop the devil listening) and make people think "about carefully language more" (more carefully about language). We spent a really interesting morning discussing all kinds of things. I asked what he did for fun and he said he made up new religions. So far he'd managed thirty eight, so we both launched into inventing some more, speaking only alphabetically. I suggested "a of worship vegetables" (a worship of vegetables) and we imagined what the hierarchy might be, perhaps with purple sprouting as divine king because of the regal colour, the Jerusalem artichoke would have to have some high status, asparagus tips as angelic warriors and the humble potato as the worshipping minions. Henry suggested a religion of colours, with bright red as a sort of supreme sun god, and "all as great nothing return to we white" (white as the great nothing we all return to). We thought about a religion based on different kinds of pain, but this had already been done by the Catholic Church.

I had some strong grass and after five or six joints we started to get sillier. A religion based on the worship of body odours, another based entirely on the worship of breasts, and another based on stupidity, with the most stupid person we knew as supreme god. It was a cross between Jim the blow up man, the safety inspector on the Titanic, and the basketball player who said "I've never had major knee surgery on any other part of my body." Henry asked if I'd ever heard of Sardanapalus. He was a philosopher who promised large sums of money to anyone who invented a new pleasure. We spent a happy lunchtime and afternoon trying to do this. One was imaginary caresses from women of our dreams, until we realised this pleasure already existed. Then we invented the pleasurable art of Gathumping – the shouting of loud nonsense words to excite pleasure. "Gersnonk!" shouted Henry. "Hubbajellyglog!" I rejoined. "Dibbersplonken!" "Jomojoncha!" Children ran away when they saw and heard us. Old ladies muttered into their beards. Only the birds twittered and celebrated with us, and the clouds rolled on joyously.

We were having a fine time when Jim arrived and surveyed our giggling dementia and the untouched paddling pool. The teat on his head started to whistle and shriek, which made me giggle uncontrollably.

"You fucking morons. My dead Aunt Fanny could have done more work," he said .

"Jim, surely you mean 'Fucking morons you. Aunt could dead done Fanny have more my work,'" I said, and rolled around on the grass weeping with laughter. Henry lay on his tummy pounding the grass and hooting. Everything was so ridiculously funny. We were still giggling maniacally an hour later when we were sacked. It seemed the funniest thing that could happen to us. I invited Henry to my place that night for more discussion and mayhem.

I'd started living in a bed-sit room in a big gothic house. Some girls refused ever to enter it because it was a castle of bad dreams, many of them mine. I had a small kitchen that I never used because things lived in the sink that could tear off an arm or leg or scoop out an eye the moment you tried to boil a carrot. I fluctuated between takeaway pure vegetarian food from health shops run by lesbians in bright scarves and wearing medieval weapons as jewellery, and industrial rubbish food. Extremes were important to me. Also in the house were two hippies of indeterminate sex who never got up, five or six students, a girl who worked in an office and brought men back to fuck savagely at lunchtimes, then another shift in the evening. I almost called the police several times when I thought she was being murdered. Also a male dancer who had evolved into a recidivist drug addict and was perfecting the techniques of the depraved in his room opposite mine. Right at the top of the house was Jack, a portly red faced gay man who worked in a fish and chip shop and whose glasses were always sliding off his nose.

Henry came round but was more subdued. It was the house. It didn't like him. It was a house of secrets and I think it suspected Henry was a mystic who could divine things it preferred to keep hidden. The house was encrypted with traces of some magical, amoral, vanished world. The shared bath had strange hieroglyphics carved into its battered enamel. I convinced myself people had lain wounded in that bath.

"Bad's happened something. And it return will." (Something bad's happened. And it will return) Then he started talking in tongues. I'd never come across this before, except for my Aussie cousin Gilly, and I don't count that because she'd drunk the best part of a bottle of Southern Comfort.

"Ageratum houstonianum ageratum mexicanum agoseris aurantiaca agoseris glauca agoseris villosa agrimonia dahurica agrimonia eupatoria agrimonia odorata." Jesus, this wasn't alphabetical speaking, this was the dog's bollocks of tongues. Straight from the plains of Jericho circa 56 AD. I sat and listened for a while, then tried to talk in tongues myself but it came out as T Rex's song Debora, "Di di di di di, Debory dub y dub and debory dub y dub oh Deborah..." Then he suddenly stopped and said he had to go, but that I should beware the return. The return of what? He just raised his eyes to the ceiling, then left. I never saw him again.

I lay in bed that night thoroughly spooked. What the hell was Henry talking about? Suddenly there were terrible noises. Banshee noises. Asylum thoughts. Malevolent shadows. Creaks that were the ancient bones of the now stirring dead. Lazarus in his binding cloth looking vainly for the grave that unearthed him. I tried chanting a mantra, *Om, Om, Om* but it echoed back at me like a rebuke. I tried prayer but was attacked by nails in hands and feet and lashing whips. Those noises. All the pain of the world in them. Pain and infinite longing for oblivion, for consciousness to cease. I got up, put an ancient lump of cheese in a sock as a weapon, and crept out into the hall. The noise was louder. Now something else, the thumping against a bed head and the wheezing of ancient bedsprings. Shit. It was only the night shift of the office girl. I went back, found a whisky bottle under the bed and swigged, then took a couple of valium and lay in the dark smoking until I drifted off into a dream about Annie's breasts bobbing under cheesecloth.

I awoke early with a hole burnt in the pillow next to my head. I must stop smoking in bed. Still, a sense of unease. The house pulsing slightly in its dissolution. I got up, brushed my teeth in the bathroom, carefully avoiding looking at the ghosts of wounded bodies in the bath, and sniffed around. There was a smell. I tracked it to the top of the house where Jack the fish and chip shop gay man lived. It was definitely coming from his room. Perhaps he was bringing his work home with him. I knocked on the door. Nothing. With an increasing sense of the ominous I realised I hadn't seen or heard him wheezing up the stairs with his bit of purloined battered cod for over a week now.

I smoked two joints in my room, and meditated on my essential godhead, but images of Annie jigging about on top of me kept intruding; these were not entirely unwelcome. I played the first side of *Gasoline Alley*, fretted a twelve bar blues on my Yamaha acoustic, and read Shelley's *Ode to the West Wind*, then went back upstairs. The smell was still there. How come I was the only sod to notice it? I could understand the humping office girl being preoccupied; she was either at work or in her room getting boned into the wall, but everyone else? I telephoned the landlord, Mr. Papadopulus. I told him there was a strange smell at the top of the house. "Mebbe you 'ave bloody bath it gone aways, eh, you stinko degeneration?" He said. I informed him that the bath was full of dark spidery rumours and the stink of golems. "Mebbe you put some bloody vim in, stink gone aways, eh?" He put down the phone.

Tenant welfare wasn't his strong point. I telephoned for an ambulance and said there might be someone ill in my house, and they said to ring back when there definitely was someone ill. Another week went by and the smell got worse and worse. Finally Mr. Papadopulus came round, not because he was worried but because Jack's rent was overdue.

I watched as Mr. Papadopulus unlocked Jack's door, then watched as he came out and vomited over the banisters. It landed with surprising ferocity on the telephone directory. I went upstairs and forever after wished I hadn't. Jack was dead on the floor. His right leg had become detached, eaten away by maggots. I turned and vomited over the banisters. It landed with surprising ferocity on the telephone itself. Police. Ambulance. Questions. Just a sad and lonely old bloke who had expired too early, and no one cared enough to even notice. His body was taken away and the Council was called to send someone to dispose of the carpet. I opened the door to Vince and Kenny, two muppets I knew from my job in Parks and Recreation. They had been employed because they were incompetent and unreliable. My heart sank. Vince also had a speech impediment.

I showed them upstairs. They went in and came running out a moment later, horrified.

"There'th a thodding leg-thing on the thodding carpet!" Vince said. Jesus Christ, they'd left the leg on the carpet.

"We ain't moving that bastard," said Kenny. "Might attack us or something."

"Might be ditheathed," added Vince.

I suggested they ring head office. Vince wanted to ring but it seemed more sensible to let Kenny do the talking. He sniffed the telephone suspiciously but said nothing. He dialled, grunted a lot then put it down.

"Spick says roll up the leg in the carpet and take it down the dump. Put it in the chemical waste bin."

"Thit!" said Vince.

With much complaining and shouting and gagging they rolled the leg up in the carpet, labelled it, and carried it downstairs. I shut the front door and lit a dozen incense sticks to disperse the stink. Then I rang the Council and got my job back. Just like that. I didn't even have to interview. It was an odd world, but at least I'd have the rent money next week. In my room I celebrated with a bowl of muesli sprinkled with goat's cheese and a glass of milk with a dash of vodka. I also smoked a joint. I liked to experiment and create new and awkward relationships between things. In fact my whole life seemed like a laboratory experiment. I certainly imbibed enough chemicals to justify this view. An hour later a knock at the door. The police. They've brought the carpet back. The leg is still inside. They obviously suspect foul play. I try to explain but they clearly don't believe me.

"Is that cannabis I can smell?" Asked one, suspiciously.

"I hope not, Officer," I say. "Surely you haven't been smoking illegal substances in your patrol car." He looks at me like barbed wire. Why do I do it? I am the author of my own ruin. I smile to show it was a joke. "No. It's incense. I'm a devotee of the Maharishi and I'm burning incense to help the soul of dear departed Jack travel to Nirvana. It's a holy thing."

The other one cocks an ear.

"What's that thumping noise?"

"It's Amanda. She works in an office."

"Sounds like someone's doing violence to her."

"She likes it like that," I say. He drops the carpet, pushes past me and bangs on the door. "Police!" Moments later a thirty something bloke runs out in his underpants, a brief case in one hand, the other waving his trousers like a flag of truce. "She was consenting!" He says and runs out and down the street. Amanda appears in a walking sexual coma, draped only in a towel, which falls to the floor, as does she, when she clocks the eaten leg on the carpet. I could see it all: Vince and Kenny couldn't bear the stink in the van, or just couldn't be bothered to go to the chemical dump, so they throw it over a hedge somewhere, with no thought of consequences. The label is still attached to the carpet. Someone calls the police. I'd had enough of this bloody leg. I step over the prostrate body of Amanda and go back to my room.

I didn't go to Jack's funeral. I suspected I might be the only one there and would find it impossibly sad. I went to his old shop and had fish and chips, then wrote a short poem to him, made a little paper boat of the poem, and launched it on the

River Lea. Goodbye Jack. I went to the library and looked through a book of plants to soothe my nerves. The words leapt out at me. Ageratum houstonianum. Ageratum mexicanum. Agoseris aurantiaca. Agoseris glauca.

Henry wasn't speaking in tongues. He'd memorized the Latin names of plants from a gardening catalogue. I suppose if God can't speak through a gardening catalogue, then no one can.

Chapter Thirteen: Return, Violent Assault, and Departure of the Hero

I was received back at Parks and Recreation with a great display of indifference. A lot of tea was drunk. A lot of arses scratched. Occasional messages from Peter were put through my letterbox at home. They were so abstruse and in the handwriting of a five year old that I didn't learn much. "Halo Steve. How are you? How is your mum? How is your dad? How is your dog? The Lord says five members in one household will be divided, three against two, and two against three. God bless you. Love Peter." He wouldn't use a telephone because he said it was a plot to get electricity in your head.

I occupied my first morning back by doing nothing, except think of clouds and the beautiful naked hips of Annie. At lunchtime I was bored listening to Mick the Dick talk about Julie's underwear and went for a walk through the woods. I was just passing a large rhododendron bush when a female voice hissed "How dare you?" I looked around and couldn't see anyone, and was just about to move away when a hand came out and grabbed me. I was pulled into the heart of the bush with surprising force and found myself staring into the demented bespectacled eyes of a middle aged woman with a hat on that looked like a spotted dick pudding. She was breathless and flushed, with a mouth like writhing eels. "How dare you?" she hissed again. She looked like Les Dawson.

"Please let me go," I said, trying to pull away, but she had one arm behind my back in a half nelson and her other hand was holding my head close.

"Let you go? How can I let you go when you're forcing your attentions on me."

"I'm not forcing anything. I just want to go."

"That's what men always say when they're about to force themselves on a poor woman. How can I stop you now you've got me in here?"

I thought of headbutting her but I'd never learnt how to do it and surmised I would probably end up breaking my own nose. She was gasping and panting. "Go on then, you beast. Get it over with. Have your way with me."

"I don't want to have my way with you," I said.

"Be rough if you have to," she said, locking her slippery oiled lips onto mine and sucking the life out of me. She'd got her skirt riding up over her thighs and had somehow managed to get my trousers around my ankles. To my horror I had an erection. "I've been watching you. I know you can't help yourself. Nothing can stop you, even though I came prepared." Prepared? What was she talking about? Suddenly there was a knife at my face, the blade about six inches long. I could see one terrified eye reflected in its steel. The word Sheffield swam into view. I did not want to lose an eye or die being raped by some demented old matron in a rhododendron bush against my will. I had a revolution to start. Enlightenment was just over the horizon. I still couldn't pronounce Nietzsche's name properly. "I promise I won't struggle any more," she said, smiling like Lucifer's mother. She nicked my cheek with the knife to show she meant business. Her thighs were like medieval stocks wrapped around my legs. She tried to force herself on top of me and grabbed my cock. I turned my mind into a cloud as she tried to force me inside her, then she over balanced backwards and I flipped over and crawled out of the bush, stood up and shuffled away, my trousers around my ankles and my cock bobbing like an enthusiastic fishing float. A woman walking towards me with a Jack Russell terrier stopped dead and fainted. I looked behind and two stout white legs were protruding from the bush at odd angles.

Back in the cabin tea room Den came in and looked at me strangely. "What have you been up to?" He asked. What was the point of saying anything? The afternoon passed in grey depression. Even the cumulus clouds didn't cheer me. The incident in the bush had scared me shitless. That evening I met Annie and told her I'd been nearly raped by a mad old harpy in a rhododendron bush with a funny hat and a knife. I told her all the gory detail and as I reached the end realised I'd made a monumental mistake. Instead of sympathy Annie was looking at me in horror. She left soon afterwards and I smoked a lot of

Bensons and contemplated the strangeness of women. I loved Annie and there was an ache in me where she had been.

My Aussie cousin Gilly came round and said she was going to Morocco in two days time. Her friend Marianne had been going with her but eloped to Switzerland with a chiropodist instead. I said I'd be Marianne. I needed to escape the memory of the monster matron in the bush. I wouldn't even wish her on Mick the Dick. Next morning I went to see Mr. Spick and quit. He said I had to work two weeks notice and I told him I'd do it when I returned. Most people steal a few things when they leave a job – pencils, a stapler, a few tools. I took a huge petrol driven mower that you sat in. I chugged it all the way home and sold it to my neighbour for twenty five quid. That would buy a few blows of kif.

The next night we flew out with Royal Air Maroc in a World War Two plane that was starting to rot inside and was decorated with peeling wallpaper bearing pictures of camels and smiling Arabs. The plane had a tendency to veer to the right so I kept leaning to the left. We arrived at an odd angle. We were staying in Agadir with a boyfriend of Gilly, Mohamet the bank manager. Marianne's Moroccan beau, Hudhud the wrestler, was waiting at the airport and wept when he saw me. He had a pair of her knickers and kept looking at them and weeping and blowing his nose on them. He was very emotional.

Agadir was not the tourist spot it is now. There was only one hotel. The streets were lively and full of dodgy and sometimes dangerous characters. Cafes with mint tea and pastries, snake charmers and wild dogs that roamed the streets at night. There were far fewer blonde women around, so Gilly with her big busty frame and long blonde curls and I caused a stir. I use the plural because with my long light hair, fair skin and light green eyes I would do just as well as a girl for the Moroccan male libido. Things went wrong almost immediately. We tanked up on mint tea, swam in the big swirling waves and I bought some kif from a one eyed man who kept spitting on his own feet. The kif was so strong I saw double. Gilly had four breasts and two heads and there were two suns beating down on us. I fell unconscious on the beach and woke up four hours later pillar box red and feeling delirious.

Mohamet took us to dinner that night to show us off. It was at a palatial house, the home of the owner of Royal Air Maroc, Agerzam, whom Mohamet wanted to poach as a customer. It was a big deal for his bank and he thought a few sophisticated friends from abroad would clinch the deal. Agerzam had a beautiful shy wife called Lalla, eyes like almonds and flawless coffee coloured skin. I'd never had sunstroke before and after two glasses of sweet white wine I knew I was going to die. Every cell in your body goes haywire. You cannot bear the thought of yourself and your own physicality is an enemy you must run and hide from in a dark corner, like a spider. An electrical charge pounds at your temples. I wondered why they are called temples. Do midgets worship and live in them, like the Numskulls in the Beezer comic, little men each with their own section of "our man's" head to oversee, looking out with tiny telescopes and plotting their ways through the day? Did the little numskulls have their own microscopic numskulls in their heads, and they in turn even smaller numskulls? This would have severe consequences for the idea of free will. I shared this thought at great, if faltering, length, with the company, but it was received with silence. I suppose cultural differences meant they hadn't read the Numskulls. A wave of hideous delirium washed over me and I left the table in search of somewhere to die.

I found an opulent bathroom with a large free standing bath in the centre. I took off all my clothes and lay in it, my legs straddled over the sides, in a desperate attempt to cool my beating body and fevered brain. I longed for cool reptilian thoughts, not this African storm of heat and nails in my head. I knew I was going to die that night but started to think it was better than this awful nightmare. I was sponging cold water over my head and scrotum and moaning when the beautiful Lalla came in. At first she was so shocked she just stared. "If I wasn't going to die in a moment I'd fall at your feet and worship your sandals and become on Arab or Berber or camel or something to show the bottomlessness of my love," I said, then threw up quite colourfully and violently.

Half an hour later Gilly and Mohamet were having heated words in his apartment. I listened outside. The words "Steve" and "idiot" and "fuck off now" seemed to occur a lot when Mohamet was talking. I decided to leave. And so it was I found myself on the streets at midnight with my travelling sports bag and nowhere to go. The first day had not gone well. I decided to stagger down to the beach and sleep there, when a low growl behind me made me turn. There were about twenty wild hungry dogs looking at me. Even the small ones looked mean. It's hard to stand your ground when you're terrified. The enemy knows you're bluffing. I backed off a few steps and the dogs trotted forward a few steps. I backed off again and they stepped forward. I was about to back off again but they were clearly tired of this game, and they all started to attack. There wasn't enough of me to feed them all. Where was the fucking angel at my shoulder when I needed him? Perhaps he was offended because I wasn't in a Christian country. When my revolution eventually started I'd make all angels ignore racial and religious and geographical boundaries. The bastards would go where I told them. If Puck could put a girdle around the earth in forty minutes, surely a big angel could muzzle a few dogs before they ripped me to pieces. Waiting for him to do so suddenly didn't seem an option. I dropped my bag and ran. Considering I was about to die I discovered I could run pretty fast. I ran to the beach and straight into the sea. It was dark. I watched the dogs on the beach barking and started thinking about sharks. Oddly enough, I felt better.

Chapter Fourteen: The Dangers of Camels and Arabs

Next morning as the sun rose it was safe to emerge from the sea. The dogs dispersed as people appeared. After a night in the water my skin had the texture of crimson bubblewrap. Gilly found me and we went for mint tea in a café. A large Arab with a head the size of a settee watched us intently. Gilly said Mohamet had cooled down and if we left it a few days he'd probably let me back in his apartment. He'd even said we could borrow his car for a few days in return for me giving him my guitar, which she said he'd already taken. This was Moroccan generosity of the highest order. We decided to drive along the coast a bit and maybe spend the night on a remote beach; she thought it might be best to avoid all human contact so that I couldn't get us into trouble. She went to get the car keys and see if she could find something to make a tent.

I closed my eyes and felt the sun burn my burnt skin. When I opened them the Arab with the mighty head was sitting with me, smiling. He put his hands together and greeted me. I did the same.

"Ahlan, blonde boy," he said.

"Ahlan. My name is Steve," I said.

"Stiff. My name Hassan like king. My eye seeing you and woman of you. 'afak to coming with me. See my house. Iss honour."

I really didn't want to go to his house.

"You saiding No is bed. You make me insulting shukran. I must killing my camel for shame."

Shit, I didn't want the death of a camel on my conscience. A minute later I was in his Mercedes speeding out of Agadir. Hassan smiled and squeezed my knee a lot. "Now you me friend," he said, "what you say shall happening, you say kill some mens I kill that persons now. God is understandings this."

We arrived in a quiet dirt road with small whitewashed houses. He led me inside one, with much ceremony and bowing. He told me he was a great fan of George Harrison and Popeye the Sailor Man. He had seen them both on television. He showed me into an immaculately clean sitting room with bright carpets and cushions and lamps, and several hookah bubble pipes. We smoked some kif. He made sweet mint tea. Then with great ceremony he took a large tortoiseshell down from the wall. It had four strings and a bridge along it. For the next half hour he played the most sublime music. Delicious little trills and flurries and pentatonic scales that hinted at Bach then moved to Robert De Visee. There was even the sitar line from 'Paint it Black' in there somewhere. It was music to delight and soothe and take you to new places. I always imagine music as a landscape and this was a place I'd glimpsed and heard in the distance, over hills, but now I was here, inside it. The silence saluted him when he finished.

"That was wonderful," I said. He beamed.

"My giff. Hassan for Stiff. Now you giff me," he said.

"Giff you what?" I asked, suspecting I knew the answer. I was wrong of course.

"The womans of you," he said.

"Gilly. She's not mine to give."

"Yiss yours. I hef her only one nights. You iss my friend I rispecting you to say I hef your womans not being the fucker do it up your back."

"Really. She's not my woman. You'll have to ask her." He laughed heartily. This was clearly a very funny joke, the idea of asking the woman if she wanted to have sex with him.

"Where she bin now, your womans?"

I told him she'd be waiting for me at the café so he drove us back there. Gilly was furious. Hassan bowed politely, took her hand and kissed it,

"I've been waiting bloody hours. I was worried. Where've you been?"

I explained that Hassan my new friend played a brilliant concert for me, and now in return he expected to spend the night with her. She gave me a look that people often give me, grabbed my hand and took me to Mohamet's car. Hassan stood staring at us, his huge head shaking with rage. Clearly I had reneged on a solemn understanding. Why was everything so difficult? As I drove us out of town in Mahomet's smart new Mercedes I had to brake suddenly. A man was wheeling a cart with two camel heads swinging from a spike. The eyes were still open and there was blood dripping from the severed necks. I had no idea camels were eaten. Or perhaps they had been executed for some crime. It was so horrifying I laughed – a reaction I often have to things that I find hideous or nauseating. Gilly looked at me in disgust. What was the point in trying to explain?

We were good soul mates and soon started chatting again. She said Mahomet had asked if I was a lunatic, and if so, had I forgotten to take my medication? I asked if she was getting on well with him, apart from me wrecking their first evening back together. She said he was an odd lover. He could only get an erection after listening to his Creedence Clearwater album. In particular, 'Up Around the Bend' seemed to do the trick and he was raring to go. She said this was OK, but she was more of a Marvin Gaye fan, so CC didn't really light up her dashboard. We drove for miles, coast on the right, desert on the left, and found a beautiful remote beach. I topped up my sunstroke for a few hours, then looked over the dunes at the desert shimmering in the heat. I thought of Peter O'Toole, *Sands of the Kalahari*, Bedouin feasts, Brian Jones coming here to record the *Pipes of Pan* at Joujouka, the Shangri Las singing 'Remember, Walking in the Sand', in those breathy, sexy voices. I decided to explore. I left Gilly improvising a tent with a wooden stake and a few sheets, and swigging from a bottle of Southern Comfort.

Walking in a real desert is a very strange experience. The geography shifts all the time, sometimes minutely, and you become less and less certain of your orientation. As someone who enjoyed mind altering experiences, and was a true expeditionary in crossing frontiers into new realms, this appealed. The sand was blisteringly hot, even through my sandals. The dunes were alive, fluid, golden. I loved sand – its clean, grainy, purity. I loved the way your feet slide into it, then how it sprays away like dry surf. I started to feel better about everything. I knew I couldn't get lost because behind me was the whole coast. All I had to do was turn around and go back the way I came. Two hours later the flaws in this simple plan were painfully manifest. I had double backed on myself about twenty times and all I could see north, south, east and west, wherever the hell they were, was more sodding sand. I hated the stuff. Why did there have to be so much of it everywhere?

I was very thirsty, my bubblewrap skin was blistering, my eyes hurt and my head was thrashing about like a drowning baby. Everywhere was identical. I had no idea which way was which, because they all looked the same. The sun was no good because it just squatted up there fatly in the middle of a cloudless sky and shone malevolently on me. I was eighteen years old and had learnt absolutely nothing, it seemed, in my whole life. There was no situation I couldn't turn into a disaster. If ever they found my dried up shrivelled body, it would be written on my gravestone: **Here lies a complete nobhead**. Stop this, I told myself. Positive thinking. I meditated and imagined a green path leading me out of the desert and, trusting to my instincts, walked long the path, knowing it would lead me back to the coast and safety. An hour later those same ancient and trustworthy instincts told me I had gone further into the desert. It was hotter and heavier. The air seemed about to burst into flames. One sandal had broken so my foot was scorching. It's very difficult to hop on sand. There are desert creatures that alternate legs so that they can cool off, but you can only do that effectively on sand with four legs. Why didn't I have four legs when I needed them? I imagined there was a big hole full of water and I drank deeply from it and put my head under to cool my boiling brain. God, it felt good. Then I saw something dark and shimmering in the distance. I stared. It was coming closer. It was Omar Sharif on a camel coming to shoot me for drinking from his imaginary water hole. I stood there, hypnotised by it.

As he got closer I realised I had imagined Omar, but the camel seemed real enough. It was traveling very fast, and showing brown and yellow teeth. I hoped it had come to save me, but in my heart I knew it wanted to kill me. Or worse – mate with me. Why? What had I ever done to him? The two severed camel heads came into my desert mind. I had laughed at them. Perhaps they were the parents of this camel and it was coming to punish me. How do you plead for mercy to a camel. I shouted "Hello! Hello! Ahlan! Ahlan!" Jesus, I didn't know they could move so fast. There was no doubt. It wanted to kill me. I turned and ran.

I reached a huge sand dune and tried to run to the top, but kept sliding down in the sand. My blistered skin was covered in sweat. It ran into my eyes so I couldn't see and the sand was sticking to me. As I fell the camel almost caught me. A great swinging rope of snotty saliva almost lassoed me. I rolled to one side, got to my feet, took a lungful of furnaced air, then started to run to the top. I thought my head would burst, my lungs catch fire. The camel was closing in again. I couldn't keep this up. With a last wrench I threw myself up to the top.

There it was. The beach. The ocean. Gilly. I kept running down, down, and into the sea, fat salty tears scalding my cheeks. Without turning I shouted "Oh Jesus! Oh God! Oh sweet fanny. Oh thank you. Gilly, Gilly, kill it! Kill the bastard! Stick a pole through the fucker's eye. No wonder they decapitate the bastards." I turned. Gilly was staring at me.

"Where is it? Where's the murdering shitface camel?" I asked when I got my breath. She looked around.

"There is no camel. What the hell have you been doing? You've been gone hours. Every time I turn my back you're off on some lunatic quest for Jesus knows what."

No camel? No camel. But of course, it was the camel who had saved my life. It made me run for my life, and that's exactly what I got. My life. Maybe my angel is a murdering bastard camel, I thought. God does move in mysterious ways.

Chapter Fifteen: A Confrontation and a Failed Revolution

Gilly and I were in our homemade tent, which consisted of one large wooden stake in the centre, and a sheet pinned out on the ground from it, like a pathetic wigwam. There was a big hole in the sheet and we looked at the stars. We were dressed because although the days were blistering, the nights were cold. I'd just told her I had an angel at my shoulder and that he whispered in my ear while I slept and that sometimes I wonder if I am just a part of his dream. She said if she'd known that she never would have come to Morocco with me. It was very peaceful.

Suddenly a noise. A snuffling, a movement, an approach. To die in a homemade tent under African stars is not the worst way to go, but I hadn't got any real momentum on my revolution going and university remained a dream down the road waiting for me. I was still unenlightened to the point at which I knew less and less each day. There was simply too much to do for me to die now. Suddenly Hassan's face eclipsed the stars and filled the hole in the tent above us. He looked very angry still.

"Hello goodbye. Smah li. Stiff, you not respecting Hassan. I make giff for you. But you taking your womans without my turns. Iss bed. No honours for me. I headbuttings you. Like this." He headbutted our tent pole and it snapped like a matchstick. Jesus, there's going to be violence.

"Hassan. I'm sorry if you got the wrong idea," I said.

"You come riding my cemel or I headbutting you." Suddenly there was a camel's head in the hole too. It seemed to be smiling shyly, revealing huge brown piano teeth. What the fuck was going on? Did Hassan want me to fuck his camel as a punishment? "You riding my cemel!" He shouted.

"I have a weak heart and I might die if I do anything obscene with your camel," I said.

"Riding my camel now today!"

"Fuck off!" Screamed Gilly. It scared me almost as much as it did Hassan. He was gobsmacked. She was a woman. She wasn't supposed to speak, let alone shout obscenities. She got right up close to him, still shouting. "Just fuck off and take your ugly camel with you, and your fucking Neanderthal ideas and your stupid beard. Fuck off back to the fourteenth century with your sheep and goats and hookah pipes and stick a French loaf up your Arab arse."

Hassan looked like a little boy about to cry. "You callings my cemel ugly. He not ugly. He fine camel boy," he whimpered, and then he and his camel disappeared. Moments later we could hear them galloping away. Gilly was some girl in a tight situation.

Next morning we swam and warmed our bones, then ate a breakfast of bananas and dates. The horrors of the night vanished with the sun. Mahomet wanted his car back this morning, but I had a hankering to go up into the mountains for a few hours. It was good to be driving a new silver blue Mercedes, the top down, the sun not yet too ferocious. The road inland snaked up a mountain. The view at the top would be worth the drive. We lived in a time when everything seemed possible and at certain golden moments it seemed the only thing worth doing was to follow your instincts. We drove several miles inland, snaking up the mountain. Suddenly there is a soldier in the road. He holds a machine gun. All I see is the khaki, a finger on the trigger, a mouth full of improvised gold teeth and a smile like a flashy piranha. There are three more soldiers standing on rocks, all with hands on machine guns and cigarettes in their mouths. Goldteeth fires a volley of shots in the air. Gunshots are terrifying when you hear them up close. Multiple terror when from a machine gun. The air crackles and echoes. Your ears hurt.

"He wants us to get out," said Gilly.

"If we get out he'll kill us. In the car he won't want to mess up the upholstery," I said.

"Who gives a fuck about the upholstery?" She asked. Goldteeth obviously did, because he was looking from Gilly to the creamy leather seats with equal lust. Gilly looked close to hysteria. I felt oddly calm, as if I'd been expecting this moment. Had I dreamt it? The soldier put the gun barrel close to my face. I could smell the cordite ghosts of bullets. He waved the barrel to indicate I should get out. We both got out and waited to be shot. He hadn't asked for our passports. This was a bad sign. It meant he didn't care who we were. I looked over at the other three soldiers to see if any of them might sympathise with two fucked up, scared travellers. One soldier was listening intently to a small hand held transistor radio. He said something to the others and they cheered. They all fired their machine guns in the air. One looked more intelligent than the others. He turned to us.

"L-yuma," he said, "King Hassan no more. Dead. We kill. We army republic. Strong army free people. Old gone. Now new." Fuck, there'd been a revolution and I hadn't even been invited. Unbelievable. I could have helped. I could have made the mint tea or written a poem or something. A revolution right under my nose and I'd been lost in a desert, completely off my head and pursued by a maniac camel. Goldteeth indicated that we were free to go and joined his comrades. Gilly got in the car, but I couldn't. I felt cheated and angry.

"Why didn't you ask me to join you? I mean, for fuck's sake, I'm with you," I shouted at the soldiers. "Vive la revolution. You could have let me in. Why didn't you let me know, you silly sods?" Gilly was looking at me strangely, as if I was digging a big hole for us to fall in, after these guys had shot us. Didn't she understand? They couldn't shoot us. We're brothers and sisters in the revolution. I took off my t shirt and tied it to a stick, stood on a rock and started waving it like a flag, then jumped off and marched up and down.

"Vive la republique!" I shouted. I was Danton and Camille and William Blake and Tom Paine and John Ball and Che Guevara. Even if I wasn't actually there for the revolution I could be a spearhead figure, an emblem of radical change. I could smoke cheroots and wear a red bandana and have a belt of silver bullets across my chest and grow a beard and have my face on t shirts in Camden market and Portobello Road. Shit, this was huge. I was vaguely aware, as I marched through the cheering crowds and salvo of cannons and waving flags and weeping girls, of the soldiers looking at me nervously, and Gilly holding her hands to her face in horror. Goldteeth pointed his gun at me. I was sweating and shouting a lot and possibly looked a little unbalanced, with my red bubblewrap skin and marching and flag waving, but this was revolution. Ordinary rules of behaviour were suspended. The other three soldiers pointed their machine guns at me. I heard several clicks. Gilly covered her eyes.

I waved the car keys. "Vive la republique! Vive Maroc army boys!" I threw the keys at the soldiers and one of them caught them. I indicated the car with a sweep of my revolutionary flag. "Here. It's yours. A gift from me to the revolution. Remember me in your prayers." The penny dropped. Goldteeth lowered his rifle and smiled broadly. The others lowered their guns and started laughing. Goldteeth got in the car and Gilly got out. Moments later we watched the soldiers driving away, laughing and joking and firing off salvos from their machine guns. It felt good to make people happy, especially revolutionaries. The good feeling lasted about three seconds.

"You gave them the fucking car!" Gilly said.

"Everyone has to make sacrifices for the revolution," I said.

"But it wasn't yours to give, and the only thing you nearly sacrificed was our lives, you fucking moron! They were letting us go until you made a complete arse of yourself and nearly got us killed."

She had a point. Several points, actually.

It was a long walk back to the beach road and a long bus ride back to Agadir; Gilly was strangely silent during the journey. Mohamet was not a happy man. There seemed little chance he would let me stay in his apartment now, despite my contribution to the revolution. He appeared keen to be rid of Gilly too. We flew home early. To cap it all, the military coup lasted less than a day before the royalist troops defeated the rebels. King Hassan hadn't been killed. It was just a propaganda broadcast. If you couldn't trust revolutionaries, who could you trust? When I started my revolution I would insist on truth as an absolute value. You can't establish a republic and heaven on earth on a tissue of lies. I tried explaining this to Gilly but she remained strangely silent throughout the whole flight. Women were still a mystery to me.

Chapter Sixteen: Cemetery Blues and Return of the Prophet

I had hidden some kif in my socks and underpants on the flight home, plus some Moroccan black hash in Gilly's case (I didn't tell her as she was being so uncommunicative) so the first few days back were spent in a beautiful haze of calm reflection and dreams. In my own mind the Moroccan revolution was by now a complete success and I had been its undisputed, if enigmatically invisible, leader. The fact that the new republic only lasted a few hours gave it romantic vigour. Things went wrong if they tried to endure. Look at France. Revolutionary ardour putrefies and itself becomes a tyranny. It was my job to keep the purity of the idea alive. I telephoned the council and got my old job back. No questions asked. Jim the blow up man was furious I'd been re-employed. He decided to punish me.

His name was Stuart. There was something seriously wrong with him and I should know, I'm an expert on human derangement and malfunction. He was short, stocky, with a face full of freckles and a nose like a piece of mucilaginous putty. His breathing was like industrial snoring. Eyes like pickled onions. Skin the colour of dirty dishwater. Nails so bitten down you couldn't see them. He had lank black hair that smelt of chip fat. Jim had paired us up for the day. We coasted along the north circular past the wastelands of Edmonton, the industrial outreaches of Enfield and were deposited at a huge cemetery near Turkey Street, where I once used to roam the streets in hope of a sighting of the delectable and glamorous Ros Banks. Social services may call it stalking but I called it love.

We were meant to mow the verges of the dead, then work our way east towards the canal and be picked up somewhere around Ponders End. The first thing Stuart did was switch off his mower and sit on a headstone to furiously pick his nose. The headstone read: IN LOVING MEMORY OF MY DEAR HUSBAND JOHN FREDERICK ABBOTT. Stuart started to deposit the fruits of his nosepicking on the word ABBOTT, and ten minutes later the dearly departed was renamed BOTT. This was going to be a long day.

I smoked a Bensons and lay looking up at the clouds. There were puffy white cumuli and higher wispy sheets of cirrus. They were going in opposite directions, a phenomenon I always found interesting. A blast of halitosis indicated that Stuart had come close. He was looking at me as if I was a lunch he would reluctantly force down.

"Summink missing in my life," he said. A brain, possibly.

"What?" I asked.

"An enemy. I need a new enemy. Fink it's gonna be you."

"You don't even know me."

"Don't matter. You're my enemy now. An' it's your fault my life is fucked up."

"Why is it my fault, Stuart?"

"'Cos you're my enemy."

I couldn't be bothered with this crap. I lit another Bensons and closed my eyes. I heard the mower start and just managed to get out of the way before Stuart minced my head. I got up. He was coming at me again. I stood behind JOHN FREDERICK BOTT's headstone and Stuart crashed his mower into it. Then a look of great vagueness passed over his face and he wandered off, leaving his chugging mower against BOTT's cracked headstone. To escape the depressing stupidity of my new work companion I took my mower for a spin among the graves. The blades almost chewed off a pair of feet. Someone was lying between two headstones. It was Peter. He was staring up, stony faced.

"Peter! How great to see you, man. What are you doing?" He turned and for a moment was the old Puckish Peter in the hint of a smile. Then the curtains closed. He looked stony again.

"Meditating," he said. "There are eight thousand, six hundred and fifty seven graves here. All those souls. Can you imagine what this place will be like on the last day? When we are judged for our sins and our own words will either save or condemn us. All these thousands of bodies resurrected."

"But it's a crematorium," I said. "It won't be a resurrection party. Just a confused heap of smoking ruin, like a giant ashtray."

"God works in mysterious ways."

"Peter, I started a revolution in Morocco. Why don't we get drunk and I'll tell you about it? I miss talking to you."

"Have you ever wondered why the Lord put the demons into a herd of pigs?"

"He was Jewish. He didn't like pork?"

"The swine is a filthy animal."

"What about Pinky and Perky? And the good pig in Animal Farm. And Miss Piggy in the Muppets. And bacon sandwiches with ketchup."

"The Lord said 'Follow me. And let the dead bury their own dead.'" He embraced me and walked away. He had a way of gliding off that made it impossible to follow him. I realised how much I'd missed him. How can the dead bury their own dead? We're back to Christianity being a celebration of zombies again. Speaking of which, the smell of rotten flesh and a chugging told me that Stuart was approaching with his mower. We eventually got to Ponders End and waited for the lorry. Stuart suddenly started his mower, put it in gear and watched it chug off into the canal. It sank with a poop poop and all that was left a minute or so later was a slick of oil and petrol and a dead duck with its arse pointing up at the grey sky.

"Why did I do that?" Stuart asked, genuinely baffled. It was no good. I had to get out of this job. The world was bright and beautiful. I wanted god and mammon, to be sanctified and blown apart; I wanted narcotic adventures and the poetry of love. I wanted to drown and be reborn in language. I had more revolutions to start, university and a lot of Nietzsche to read. Someone must have been listening. When I got home there was a telegramme for me. I'd never had one before. I spent a lot of time, especially at work, reading the music press – *NME, Disc and Music Echo, Melody Maker, Rave, Fabulous.* This telegramme was a peach from *Disc and Music Echo.* I'd entered a competition about Rod Stewart and the Faces and had won a trip to the States to see them on their Rock and Roll Circus tour, with Free and John Baldry.

I resigned from Parks and Recreation and rang Annie to ask her to go out with me before I went to America. Her mother told me never to call again. I said I loved Annie and she told me I didn't know the meaning of the word. I asked which word she meant and she put down the phone. A few days later I was on a plane to Florida. A friendly steward brought me a bottle of champagne and I sat drinking it and looking down on the clouds. This is how the gods travelled, with clouds for company. Apollo chasing across the sky in his fiery chariot. I thought I was in paradise but I was flying into the eye of a fire. I wasn't Apollo; I was Icarus and already too close to the sun. I would also be an unwilling Orpheus.

Chapter Seventeen: Rock and Roll Circus

For a few years the Faces were the best live band around. Laddishly wasted, riding their luck, they carved out a special niche in popular music. It was as if the Music Hall had found a way into rock and roll. Life was a carnival of celebration, excess and fun. If you turned up early you may well find Stewart in the bar topping up on port and brandy, wearing pillar box red velvet trousers that didn't like his ankles. Sometimes they didn't play well, depending on how drunk they were, but it didn't matter. The concert was still a spectacle. When they did play well it was sublime. I'd had some of my best nights at their shows. I woke up in a ditch outside Walthamstow Town Hall with a fractured nose. I found myself on the roof of the Roundhouse at 5 am with a giant plastic banana called Chiquita. I woke up wearing a woman's ball gown in a Watford warehouse. You get the picture. They kicked footballs into the audience and partied onstage. There was no pretentiousness; self indulgence was a thing to be mocked, and for a few hectic years they kept each other in check like this. Long boring solos or artful lyrics were outlawed and seriousness had to be fun too. In the early seventies, after *Maggie May* and *You Wear it Well*, Rod Stewart was like god in America, a spiky haired long legged cockerel in ridiculous outfits and an assortment of women's scarves. As the behaviour got more outrageous, so did the clothes. As Stewart later said, "We didn't get drunk and go out with old tarts because we thought it was cool, we did it because we wanted to."

I sat in a small caravan near the stage entrance to Tampa Stadium and listened to the final barking chords of *Sweet Little Rock and Roller*. Then the band was there, sweaty and adrenalin high after the concert. Ronnie Lane, the bass player, wanted a photograph of the band beating me up for the music press. Back at the hotel a girl called Candy asked me to marry her and take her to England. A black dancer called Charlie said he wanted to dance his way to Africa. There were a lot of amphetamines and strange desires and cigarettes. Glass was broken. Flesh was tested to the limits. Two middle aged men started fighting after an argument over whose daughter had slept with Rod Stewart the night before. I don't think Rod could remember. I was meant to be sharing a room with a roadie, but his sexual habits were apparently so ghastly that it was decided I should have my own room thereafter. Rock and roll touring was clearly a very serious business and almost as deranged as working for the council.

The next night we stayed in the Castaways Hotel on Miami Beach. Glass was broken. Starbright clothes were worn. Flesh was tested to the limits. I hadn't really slept for two days and was beginning to look like a hippy alien – long haired, saucer-eyed and thin. Billy Gaff, the manager, a small, anxious wheeler and dealer, liked me and one day I sat in his room while he made phone calls, then he turned and looked at me.

"How long are you here for?" He asked.

"Just a few days," I said.

"No. Not happening. You don't come all the way to the states and go straight home, and not even see the big apple."

"But I don't have any money."

"I'm making you part of the tour. I won't pay you anything, but you'll get all your hotel bills paid, travel and food. OK?"

I thought about it for two seconds.

"OK. But what shall I do?"

He thought for a moment. "Your job is to sit on stage for every performance keeping the wine cooled for the band. This is a very important job. Are you up to it?"

I was. My job was very simple. I sat at the side of the stage with a bucket keeping the Blue Nun wine chilled to the right temperature, which meant chucking in a lot of ice when the first lot had melted. Blue Nun, now a thing of derision in wine circles, was considered the dog's bollocks of vino to the tour. The first night, at a football stadium in Georgia, I sat stage left and kept the wine nicely cooled. Ronnie Wood and Ronnie Lane smiled at me occasionally and I'd hand them a bottle for a swig. Rod preferred his in a plastic cup. Between numbers I would scuttle across and replenish Mac's plastic cup at the piano and Kenny's at the drums. I felt as if I might have found my vocation in life. All went well until the end of the show when Free were invited back onstage for a final joint rendition of *I know I'm Losing You.* Free drummer Simon Kirke's drum kit was dragged on where I was sitting. I clutched the wine bucket and it was so cramped I had to curl up into the bass drum and duck because a couple of cymbals were above my head.

Simon Kirke was a very muscular, physical drummer who didn't spare the skins. The first thunder from the bass drum rattled my head and the first clash of the cymbals made my ear drums scream. Five minutes later I thought I'd gone completely deaf and my teeth throbbed and threatened to jump from my head. When the number finished I was helped to my feet and staggered across the field to the dressing room. Ronnie Lane started telling me a joke and I couldn't hear a thing, so I just laughed anyway. His expression changed to a snarl and someone held him back from hitting me. When my hearing returned I discovered he was telling me about his Nan dying. I apologized and he said it was fine but that he would probably beat me up anyway some time.

Chapter Eighteen: Stoning the Pilot and Missing the Mountain

We then went to Georgia and Carolina. Families paid for their daughters to travel with us, perhaps in the hope they'd get bedded by the band. I guess it would make interesting dinner party chat in certain Bohemian circles. If the concert was in a sports stadium, we'd kick the floodlights back on afterwards and have a game of football, which made a change from indoor sports. I lay in bed one morning playing chess with myself when I heard a strange noise coming from the shower. Paul Kossoff, the soon to be dead guitarist with Free, had obviously been in there all night and had just woken up. He walked out without a word. There was already a lostness about him when he wasn't playing guitar.

"You all right, Paul?" I asked.

"I'm walking out of this room," he said, and did just that. He had a very literal take on things.

On a small private plane to Georgia two of the band and a bevy of roadies smoked a lot of serious dope and we suddenly realised that either the dope was stronger than we thought or the plane was upside down. The interior was just one cabin for pilot and passengers, and the pilot had been breathing in a lot of what we had exhaled for the past half hour. He had a faraway smile on his face and said his mother was an angel. I told him I had an angel at my shoulder. We were enjoying sharing our experiences of angels, despite the fact that a mountain seemed to be heading towards us at great speed.

"Shit!" shouted a roadie, which was apposite as several people had done just that. Someone grabbed whatever it is that steers a plane and pulled it about a bit and the mountain stopped hurtling towards us. There were a lot of frantic voices on the radio but the pilot and I laughed and told them to chill out. My memory is that the angel at my shoulder calmly sat at the controls, flipped switches, scrutinised controls and landed us with divine smoothness on a small private aerodrome, then vaporized to avoid public attention. I looked in vain for him as we tried to explain to the police why we'd made an unscheduled landing. I hadn't slept for three days now.

At a huge park in Carolina John Baldry opened the show. Six feet seven inches and wearing a holy man's white shirt and trousers. He started and no one listened. A lot of shouting and eating and drinking and chatting, but mostly people ignored him. It didn't seem fair. Without him there would be no Rod Stewart – he'd given him his first serious job and a hell of a lot of encouragement. He stopped and left the stage. Moments later he returned with a chair and a plastic cup full of brandy. He sat and started to sip the brandy and chat about anything that came into his head: the weather, great blues musicians he'd known, songs he liked. By the time he'd finished the brandy everyone was listening. He'd created an intimacy with the crowd. Now they liked him. He stood up and launched into *King of Rock and Roll.* Now they loved him. The Faces came on and a lot of footballs were kicked and a good time was had by all. Afterwards a lot of wine was drunk and a lot of pills popped and Baldry made a lot of lewd suggestions to Ronnie Lane about sucking cocks.

I hadn't slept for four days. I was unravelling fast and loving every moment of it. Burn brightly. There were interesting philosophical debates at breakfast:

(Rod Stewart slightly bleary eyed with a young lady)

ROD STEWART I haven't slept all night.

STEVE Sleep deprivation can be as good as drugs.

ROD STEWART No. Just means you're knackered.

STEVE As good as sex?

ROD STEWART No.

STEVE As good as sleep? Marmite soldiers? Trench foot?

ROD STEWART Fuck off, weirdo. I'm tired.

I was challenging the boundaries of thought and pleasure, the endurance of the human body, the frontiers of indulgence. I think everyone else was just having a bloody good time. I tried to tell anyone who would listen, and no one did, that while John Lennon was moaning about the CIA I applauded their ingenuity because they were busy developing some of the mind altering chemicals that would amuse, enlighten and destroy much of my generation: LSD, mescaline, psilocybin, PCP, and various 'truth' serums which often created lifelong psychoses. They also sold opium, cocaine, crack, and helped a generation of war veterans to become hopeless addicts. For a dealer that is gold plated success beyond anything Parks and Recreation could dream of. I was becoming a full bloodied conspiracy theorist and serious revolutionary, especially after my spectacular success in Morocco, and I can honestly say that no one on the Rock and Roll Circus tour had the slightest interest. This was fine by me because it gave me time to refine my ideas without the messy intrusion of other people's opinions.

Chapter Nineteen: Unravelling in the Apple

By the time we got to New York three weeks later I had practically disintegrated, but my revolutionary theory was more robust. I knew that the weaker I became the stronger the theory was in direct proportion. I had absolutely no logical evidence for this belief, nor much of an idea how it would trigger a revolution. My increasingly powerful memories of marching at the head of a spiritually enlightened, radical, cheering populace in Morocco were a great comfort and had solidified into photographic reality.

I was staying at Loew's Regency hotel in Park Avenue. My room was paid for the next three days but I only had three dollars left and it would cost a packet to get to JFK. I couldn't remember the last time I ate. The tour was over, the circus had left town. Rod and the Faces were back in England. I had one tab of LSD left and, in the absence of food, took it. Two hours later I was sitting in a coffee shop watching the bass player of Free, Andy Fraser, have breakfast or lunch or dinner with a skinny, impossibly beautiful girl. He asked how I was and I said I was imagining eating his waffles. He offered them to me and I said food was all in the mind. He shrugged and carried on eating. I wondered why I'd said such a pretentious arsehole thing when I was actually starving, so I went over, sat down, and started eating his waffles with my fingers. The girl looked alarmed as I started to eat her club sandwich with the waffles. I told her she had eyes like planets and one day would give birth to a giant salamander who would speak in tongues and bring revolutionary zeal to all living and dead mammals in downtown Manhattan. Very soon afterwards I was asked to leave. It was the last food I'd have for three days.

I realised the LSD had probably been a mistake when I saw King Kong on top of the Empire State Building in a pair of giant y-fronts shouting in Chinese. It didn't seem a good idea to tell anyone, knowing that people were prone to paranoia and anxiety when you told them the truth of things. Now I started to think about it, the realisation occurred that I might be the only sane, rational person in this city of endless night, city that never sleeps, the apple that makes maggots of all. I started to hear the Doors song 'People are Strange' floating down Madison Avenue, the words like living harpies writhing just above the heads of passersby:

People are strange when you're a stranger
Faces look ugly when you're alone
Women seem wicked when you're unwanted
Streets are uneven when you're down
When you're strange
Faces come out of the rain
When you're strange
No one remembers your name
When you're strange
When you're strange
When you're strange
No one remembers your name.

Shit. Suddenly I couldn't remember my name either. This song was powerful voodoo. How come no one else could see or hear the words? I suddenly realised everyone was only pretending not to notice them. I had to be careful, I was in the heart of a powerful conspiracy, but who was behind it? The CIA? God? Donald Duck? The possibilities shuttered through my mind like images on a fruit machine. And what did they want from me? It struck me with the force of lightning they knew about the revolution I was going to start and were now out to get me. I would have to be very cunning. On the face of it I was just like any other skinny, long haired, half starved, nineteen year old sweaty lunatic with mad eyes who had taken a monster tab of acid and hadn't washed in a few days, strolling down Madison Avenue, but inside I was plotting my next move. First, I needed to remember my name. That would be a strong start. At least then I would know exactly who it was starting this revolution.

But how many were involved in the conspiracy? The President? Maybe it even stretched back to Parks and Recreation. Maybe George hadn't swallowed rat poison at all because he simply couldn't cope with his own teeming, confused life;

perhaps he'd been on the verge of telling me about them, whoever they were, so they murdered him and faked his suicide. It all started to fit. My friends had been sent mad, or driven into the arms of dubious gods, or all murdered, so they couldn't tell me the truth.

I needed to know my name before I could continue my expedition into this heart of dark intrigue. I looked for clues in shop names: *Clemente & Polo.* Neither of those rang a bell. *Crate and Barrel.* No. *Ann Taylor.* Was I in fact a woman? *Lana Marks.* Another woman's name; what could it mean? Suddenly I thought of Annie. She was my love. She would know my name. I would have to ring her if I couldn't find out. *Calvin Klein*? The name seemed familiar but it didn't feel right on my tongue. *Roberto Cavalli. Jimmy Choo. Giorgio Armani. Ralph Lauren.* These names were familiar, but were they mine or the enemy's? *Gucci. Cartier. Prada.* This was driving me crazy. I decided to randomize my name from the clues I'd been given. From now on I would be *Giorgio Lana Ralph Prada Gucci.* I said it aloud and it suddenly felt right. Perhaps that's who I really am, I thought. It felt momentarily good to know exactly who I was. I realised my new names were an anagram for *Guard Rigid Anal Hog Capo Clap* but that didn't matter. It was still a fine name.

I passed a woman with some sort of cauliflower growing out of her head. It occurred to me that as soon as there is life there is disease. Something lives and instantly something else wants to attack it, from without or within, and new diseases are constantly inventing themselves. Apparently syphilis began when Christopher Columbus fucked a sheep against its will. Now I had discovered the modern disease: diminishing thought. It was as if everyone's skull was made of glass as they passed me and I could see inside. There were the usual bobbing congestions of lusts, wants, needs, deceptions and disappointments, but what I could see with chilling clarity was that someone, or something, was systematically fencing in everyone's thoughts. The brain pan was merely a bubble of trapped insects going insane with frustration. The sound was horrendous, the frenetic activity futile, a pointless cacophony. Thought had been stripped of all instrumentality. Soon, no one would be able to even conceive of changing the world – all thought was collapsing into a mere graceless babble. People would watch TV more and more until TV was watching them in an inane symbiosis. Knowledge was being replaced by information, wisdom by advertising. Dissent would be a vanishing memory, opposition an endangered species, change become extinct. We would all be slaves to nothing much and servants of our own futility.

All this was as plain as day to me and I had to do something. The world had to be awakened from its torpor, like a sleeping Princess, otherwise our heroes would be chat show hosts and advertising jingles, money mad celebrity morons and caged monkeys, instead of the mad gods, dangerous idealists, wild animals, self-destructive angels and beautiful poets of the hungry heart and haunted soul, that we should aspire to.

I had to kick start my revolution today. Now. People had to know what was being done to them. I, *Georgio Lana Punani Prada Banana* or whatever the fuck my name was, would tell them. I started at the zoo in Central Park. Animals were always more receptive and sensitive and intelligent than people. A polar bear listened and immediately understood, but could only express his anger in a stressed frenzy of underwater swimming in filthy, shit coloured water. I turned around and Peter was beside me, looking in horror at the water.

"What's the matter?" I asked.

"I'm terrified of water," he said.

"Peter, what are you doing here?"

"I'm not here. You are."

The polar bear was going crazy. I looked back and Peter had gone. I banged on the glass to try and free the bear but was ejected from the zoo. I whistled my message to the birds and caused panic in the trees. I poured my heart out to a poodle whose perfumed owner scuttled her away in terror. I tried to shepherd the wind to some radical purpose and the wind whispered back that everything was dismayed by my message, and they, whoever they were, had already dispatched their agencies of destruction and weapons of control to hunt me down.

Where could I start now? I walked north into the depths of Harlem. In those days, no skinny white kid walked into Harlem unarmed unless they had a powerful death wish, but I had work to do. The brothers might understand what I was saying. And if I died in the attempt at least I'd know I tried.

Chapter Twenty: Say You Want a Revolution

Harlem had darkened under the spectre of riots in the mid sixties. Poverty and neglect kills the heart as well as the body. The Black Panthers agitated for change through violence; Max Stanford, a Black Panther, declared that the United States "could be brought down to its knees with a rag and some gasoline and a bottle." The assassinations of Malcolm X and Martin Luther King Jr. created a despair of anger and frustration. There was burning, looting and murder. When their dreams die people can get ugly. The worst period in Harlem was in the early 70s because those Harlemites who could afford to, got out to safer areas and what was left were the poorest and least hopeful. Infant mortality increased to a staggering 42.8 per cent; over 90 per cent of kids didn't attend school; rape and drug addiction were local pastimes; illness, ever the bedfellow of poverty, became rife and drugs replaced food. Houses and shops were boarded up, creating a ghetto of shutters and secrets and bitter hopelessness. The local economy collapsed and most cash that did come into the area came from the illegal numbers game. Children carried Uzis and Glocks and the word 'respect' became an absurd excuse to use them. Children strutted as crack/cocaine dealers and users, bodyguards and killers, but the Italians and Hispanics had a stranglehold on drug sales so blacks couldn't even profit much from their own addictions. Murder was commonplace. Human life was simply a bartering tool in turf wars. Children had children of their own; girls were known as 'dogs.'

The worst part of Harlem was the "Bradhurst section" between Adam Clayton Powell Jr. Boulevard and Edgecombe, from 139th Street through 155th. Skyscraper crime rates, collapsing tenements, waist high rubbish on some streets piled against doors and in vacant lots, rats the size of alligators, and the whiff of violence everywhere. Danger and desolation hung over it like a giant spider web. It was into these streets that I walked on a May morning to start my revolution that would change the world. A lot of people did double takes, then just stopped and stared at me. A couple of rusting beaten up chevvies slowed and the drivers gawped. My plan was to just walk about a bit and see what happened – not brilliant, but very open. It didn't take long for things to happen.

Suddenly a man was in front of me. He seemed to just drop from the sky. Maybe he was a prophet or something. If so, he was a mighty hedonistic one – he smelt of meths and stale sweat and looked like a red-eyed Huddie Leadbetter – big and rangy but full of hard times.

"Now you ain't gonna let me pass a liquor store without buying me a drink, is you, white boy?" He said. We were in a row of boarded up tenements. Shops were a distant memory in this wasteland.

"There isn't a liquor store," I said.

Suddenly a black hand holding a bottle in a brown paper bag shot out from between two planks of wood nailed to a window. "Fine fruits of the vine, my man," the hand said.

"How much?" I asked.

"How much you got?" the hand asked.

"Three dollars," I said.

"To you, my man, three dollars."

I gave the hand my last three dollars and then gave the bottle to the black guy. He took a swig and wiped his grizzled mouth. The hand disappeared back into the tenement.

"Name's Curtis." He held out a hand. I gave him mine.

"Harpo Gucci Bandana Lorna Georgio."

He looked at me strangely.

"My reckoning, boy, whatevva yo' name is, ya' got about one minute get yo' skinny white ass outta here in one piece," he said. His timing was immaculate. A minute later I was surrounded by young blacks with red headbands and dirty jeans. They were all skinny with too bright eyes, except for one who was fat and ugly. He had a knife with a nine inch blade. He waved it in my face. He wanted to split me from chops to chutney. The acid was still carpet bombing my brain so I decided not to mention the llama standing next to him and smiling at me, in case it wasn't there.

"What ya' doin' on my patch, white boy?" He asked.

"I decided to start a revolution here. In this street. Next to this pile of garbage. "

Fatty smirked. The rest of the gang smirked.

"Ya' fuckin' my ass, white bitch. Ya' gonna start a revolution on my patch?"

"Where is your patch, exactly?"

"This my patch, muthafucka. Over otha' side of the block belong to the Bloods who part of the Crips. Round one fifty five the Chaplains under Macey the Magician. One four seven to one four nine the Skinny Sinners and here where ya' got yo' white feet is mine, Crazy Horse, captain of the Diablos. Any mo' questions befo' I blade ya' down the snatch?"

"It's a pretty crappy patch to be Captain of. Why don't you find somewhere nicer? With a bit of garden or something." This was stupid, but it gained me ten seconds silence as they looked at each other in astonishment. I decided to plough on. "Nietzsche, and I think you pronounce it like 'tea-cher', said you have to live dangerously, and one must have chaos within oneself, to give birth to a dancing star. That's part of what I want to tell you – that all this chaos can be useful, it's a sort of cosmic energy. The other thing is that there's a conspiracy against us all – me, you, everyone. Our thoughts are being caged and eventually we'll be tame morons. I mean - it's already started with you. All you can think about is a little turdy piece of street that even the cockroaches wouldn't pay rent for. And why do you dress like a music hall carpet bagger? I know you're poor and you got a reputation to keep up, and the street is where authority is tested and reputations made, but Jesus Christ, what's the point? There's loads of you. Why don't you join together and march on City Hall? I'll go with you. I did it in Morocco. I could write a poem for you."

I could see one or two of the gang were actually listening, but Crazy Horse wasn't interested; I felt a whumph in my stomach and thought: this is it, I've got a knife gone right through me and out the other side. I lay on the floor as Crazy Horse took off my sneakers, the only thing worth stealing apart from my denim jacket, and looked at my midriff. No blood. It had been a punch. I was too winded to speak. Crazy Horse felt my pockets to see if there was a wallet, which there wasn't, gave me a kick in the groin and spat on me."

"I see yo' skinny white arse roun' here again I kill ya'." He wobbled away, followed by the rest of the Diablos. Curtis helped me to my feet. I was violently sick over a pile of rubbish where someone, or something, had already been sick a few hours before. I lurched forward as someone pushed me from behind. I turned over to see another black gang looking down on me, although one or two Mexican looking guys were among them. The front man was exceptionally tall with a wispy beard, an ear ring through his nose and a bowler hat.

"Wha' the fuck ya' doin' on my patch, white ass?" He said.

"I thought it belonged to Crazy Horse and the Diablos."

He laughed and the others joined in. They were all under twenty.

"That fat muthafucka'? You is kiddin' me. Diablos a box o' fruits is all. This mine. We the Bishops and I, mah man, am John the Baptist." He opened his Jacket to reveal a large grey gun tucked in his jeans. "And when I baptize some muthafucka they stays baptized, yaknow what I mean?" He checked to see if I had a wallet, then pulled off my jacket and gave it to one of his lackeys. "That fat piece o' shit Crazy Horse is the lowest o' the low."

"I've worked in Parks and Recreation. I've seen how low life can get," I said.

"Parks and Recreation. Wha' the fuck you saying?"

"There's a conspiracy," I said. "They're trying to control us. They do it through television and the press and institutions and infecting our thoughts. They feed us lies. We could stop it so easily. We just have to say No, and keep saying it. No, we've had enough." I wasn't feeling particularly lucid after being starved, exhausted, beaten up and having a head full of acid.

"You think I listen to some white muthafucka?" Said John the Baptist.

"I could be black, with a bit of practise," I said. He took out his gun and pointed it at my face. I passed out.

Chapter Twenty One: Still Going Revolution Crazy in Harlem

I woke up next to a trash can just outside Central Park. It was dusk. As well as losing my sneakers, my denim jacket and my mind, my t shirt had also gone. I had clothed half of Harlem in one day, which wasn't bad. How did I get here? I thought that the angel at my shoulder had descended in a fiery chariot, destroyed the gangs in a hail of brimstone and diamond arrows and rescued me from certain death. Or possibly Curtis put in a good word for me, or they didn't think me worth killing, and they just drove here and dumped me outside their territory. This seemed likelier.

A cop was walking towards me, so I staggered to my feet and into the park. I pushed my way into a large bush and tried to coax, then bully, the black flitting harpies from my mind. After I managed that I spent an age bullying, then coaxing out the circus dwarves and mythical beasts who had pitched their big top in the amygdala and orbitofrontal cortex of what used to be my brain. That acid had made a valiant attempt at reconstructing my whole biology, and was now subsiding into mere hysteria and lobular plumbing. With any luck I'd be back to my normal self in, say, three or four lifetimes. Where was my angel? Where was Annie? Where the fuck was I? More to the point, who was I? My name had slipped away again. I was too tired to be crazy for now. The bush was my mother and father. I slept.

I woke up, possibly the next day, with a powerful nectar of Armageddon in my nostrils. My life is an experiment that is going disastrously wrong, I thought. I hated America. It was full of sound and fury, signifying nothing, but I was a revolutionary expeditionary in search of enlightenment and global change. A name floated into my mind. Dick. I said it aloud but it didn't feel right. Then from nowhere came the word Steve and I knew I was halfway home. Remembering this simple nomenclature topped me up with new confidence. There was only one thing to do – go back to Harlem and finish what I'd started. Paranoia is an excellent trigger to action because you perceive everything clearly and quickly and act spontaneously on it.

As I strolled half naked down 142nd Street in Harlem half an hour later Curtis looked up from the gutter where he sat holding his battered head. He looked a hundred years older. The evil juice was killing him quickly. His rheumy eyes widened as he realised it was me and he started shaking his head in disbelief.

"Wha' the fuck, whitey? They let ya' go yes'day, boy. T'day they eyeballs ya back they kill ya'."

I sat next to him.

"It's like this. I had a revelation in a bush last night. I realised Christ's teachings are biological suicide. Love thine enemy as thyself is complete bollocks. The mouse embraces the cat and minutes later is dead. The deer lies down with the lion and is suddenly lunch. The fish loves the fishermen and is supper. It's as if Christ wanted everyone to become lemmings. And this is the point – we have to know who our enemies are, then get them before they get us. Loving your enemy is a deeply flawed doctrine."

Curtis wasn't listening; he was looking down the street.

"Here come the night," he said.

Crazy Horse was wobbling purposefully towards me with six of his gang behind him. He already had his knife out. He started shouting when he was twenty feet away. "I tell ya I see ya here in my hood I kill ya'. You ain't never goin' home now, whitey, 'cept as chopped liver." These urban warriors got straight to the point. A battered rusting red chevvy screeched to a halt on the other side of the street. John the Baptist jumped out and came straight for me. His eyes were dancing fire as he leaned in close: "I give ya'a reprieve, muthafucka, an' you got the brass t' come back in my territory. Man, ya nat'rally stupid or ya' take classes?"

"I came back 'cos I've got a message."

"Who from?"

"Shelley."

"Who the fuck Shelley? I don' need no message from no bitch."

"That's a grammatically meaningless double negative. Shelley's a poet. He said we could live sceptreless, free, uncircumscribed, but equal, unclassed, tribeless, and nationless, exempt from awe, worship, degree, every person the king over himself."

"Wha' the fuck that mean?" Clearly Shelley's revolutionary vision was failing to reach across the ages to John the Baptist in Harlem.

"Hey man, I like the bit about dudes being kings over their selves. Like me," said Crazy Horse, forgetting for the moment he was going to kill me.

"Who give a waving dick what you think, fat bitch," said John the Baptist. "And get the fuck off my street."

Crazy Horse's eyes squidged up in malice. "Yo' street? I don' think so, Baptist boy. Ya' trespassing on sacred ground."

"This street's a toilet," I said. "It's ridiculous that anyone would want it. We have to go outside. To them. Challenge them."

"Who – the Holy Beggars? Their patch is 154th. I ain't messin' with those spik assholes," said Crazy Horse.

"No, not another gang. Them. Outside. People who run things. Everywhere. The leaders. They're deranged. They are mentally ill. We have to capture them and lock them up or kill them before they do us any more damage. All this is their fault."

"Oh yeh, I see to them muthafuckers, but first I take you out," and Crazy Horse moved towards me with his knife.

John the Baptist took out his gun and fired a shot in the air. A gunshot is a terrible sound. The air echoes and everyone stops breathing. Your eardrums rattle and hurt. "Anybody waste that skinny white bitch, I do it. This my hood," said John.

Crazy Horse slashed with his knife and caught John across the cheek. The skin opened like an envelope flap. After a moment's quiet there was pandemonium. The two gangs were at each other like rabid dogs. Suddenly the tenements were rotten logs leaking woodlice. Teenage kids, even little kids, were coming from everywhere and joining in. This wasn't a playground, it was fighting that went for the jugular. It was serious violence. What was I, a self confessed coward, doing here? Suddenly a large shaking pair of hands reached out from a boarded up window and yanked me off my feet and inside, splintering the wood. I landed on the floor in the darkness. It was the hands I spoke to yesterday – they'd saved me because I was a customer, I suppose. Now there was a pair of huge bloodshot eyes above the hands.

"You one crazy white scarecrow. Now you git outta here afore they come looking."

I groped about. The stench was terrible: dampness, tobacco smoke, stale sweat, urine and shit. I was aware of slumped figures in corners. An explosion outside but I wondered if it was in my head. I tripped over a lump and it groaned. As I fell my hand landed on something soft and unpleasant. I couldn't breathe and started to panic. Someone laughed maliciously in the dark. I ran blindly straight into a wall, then felt my way along slowly. "Help," someone said. It sounded like a child. I kept moving. A huge sack covered what felt like a door handle. I yanked and pulled and it wheezed open onto a back yard full of decaying rubbish. A large rat stood on its hind legs eating something made of flesh. The rat looked at me, unafraid; after all, I was on his turf. Beyond in the street people were running, some towards the battle on the next street, some escaping it. A black middle aged woman ran past, holding her hand to one eye, blood rivering between her fingers. She was moaning soft and low like a lullaby of death.

I did this. I am the cause. It's my fault. Everything is my fault, I thought, as I heard more gunshots and breaking glass, screaming and shouting. I'd been told that the police only come afterwards, to clear up. They wouldn't risk it now. Who could blame them? It was war.

Chapter Twenty Two: Thrown Out of America

I wandered out of Harlem, through the police cars that were already cordoning off the area until the worst of the violence had exhausted itself. A few cops looked at me curiously: naked down to the waist, socks in shreds, emaciated and filthy, but I was beyond caring. I'd had the absurd sense that everything was possible, and now the wreckage of my pathetic idealism lay behind me, torn and bleeding in the damned streets of Harlem. Given that I was so hopelessly incompetent at life, how had I managed to cause so much mayhem and destruction? I came across the Atlantic to be with a fun-loving drunken rock band and I'd caused a war.

I stopped in the middle of Fifth Avenue, cars streaming and honking both ways past me. I didn't care. I looked down and seemed to see myself in bits on the road – an eye, hair, a leg, dreams and poems and books, all skewed like discarded pieces of Meccano. I thought – I have torn my own life to pieces and now stand in the road looking at them and wondering what sort of machine I can make if only I can work out how to connect them. A dysfunctional and tragic machine created only to be abandoned.

I turned right onto West 57th then trudged down Sixth Avenue towards Times Square, people getting out of my way. I was a stranger to my own breed, a ghost to myself, and a spectator at my own ruin. The spaces that had been opened up in my mind now filled with a great wash of realisation that most of what I had thought was nonsense. Mostly I was sick of God and he'd probably had more than enough of me too. Who did he think he was, fucking us about like this? Christianity, and perhaps all religion, is based on creating terror. People are frightened of transgressing, so they make up arcane and ridiculously complicated laws and beliefs, in the hope they can hide in the thicket they have themselves created, along with the big bogeyman to punish them. It is a faith which delights in the disaster of others. The Bible is a big book of men looking for forgiveness and protection and revenge, but there is nothing to forgive, and no one to punish or protect you. God suits the powers that be, I realised. It keeps people tame, and that's what they want us to be - digging our own graves in fear and mediocrity.

I sat down on the pavement and wept. I was probably there for hours because when I looked up it was dusk and everything had changed. I was stuck. My body had rooted through the concrete. A cat's paw of terror caressed my spine and I thought: on Times Square I can connect nothing with nothing. Wei la la. I am moored in a vast, fissured prison. Underground pipes spurt noxious gases that poison us. This city is full of strange animals and creatures that, when they move, take the space they occupied with them, and we will eventually choke on the remaining nothingness. Winking lights are the jewelled eyes of tree frogs. The night is a curtain of fire, a disorderly tumour formulated by chaos, lacerated by toxic fireworks. People are foraging bags of greed. Beauty is always tragic, always precarious, always destroyed by people. The last English wolf falling to a hunter's arrow, the last honey bee choked in a virus, the last tiger bred to be shot by a rich man, the last lemur netted by the indifferent curious, the last cuckoo silenced by a chainsaw. This city is a vast net catching our very souls. We choke on ourselves. Our desires are rapacious, our dreams consume themselves. A sudden unbearable knowledge that everything is alive. Sun. Sky. Sand. And the pulse that quickens it all is indifferent. Airbrush away the words and the horrible truth is always there, waiting like a fatal illness.

I knew I was coming to the end of myself, and saw that I would have to dissolve in the darkness that waited like a hunter at twilight. Then I looked up and he was there, no longer at my shoulder, but looking down at me sternly. I had disappointed him, but at least he had come. I might yet be rescued.

Minutes later I couldn't understand why my angel was wearing a cop's outfit, driving me in a NYPD car and had a Bronx accent, but there it was. Something in the car stank, and I realised it was me. My mum would be horrified, not that I had destroyed myself and half of New York, but that I didn't have on clean socks and pants.

"What's your name?" I asked.

"Al," he said. Funny name for an angel.

"I thought you'd be called Gabriel or Michael, and be in a sort of chariot thing, and with long blonde hair like Brian Jones."

"You're fucking weird, kid." A swearing angel. What was left of my mind boggled. I was in the back seat and I saw in the mirror that my face was filthy and bloody and that I was crying helplessly. Everything was in Al's hands now. He was looking at me strangely.

"You're not my angel, are you, Al?"

"Fucking fruitcake limey kid."

Half an hour later I was being interviewed by Sergeant Joe Griselde. He was heavily pockmarked and scowled a lot at the report form he was filling in laboriously.

"You can't remember where you were staying, you got no clothes or money, no form of ID and no passport on you. That makes you a vagrant." It seemed a fair and accurate description. "Anything at all you can tell me so I know what the hell I can do with you, other than hose you down in the shower room?"

I thought hard. "All I can say is; sorrow is the most sensitive of all created things. I live in a state of enlightened mystification. My personality barely holds together. Sometimes I think all I can do is tear myself to pieces and scatter them like confetti over the lives of everyone I know."

Joe looked at me.

"Listen, kid, I got a full blown riot in Harlem. All leave cancelled. We even got the army going in. So some brain-screwed limey fuck up on legs who don't know his ass from a hole in the wall is not big potatoes. You are a footnote here. I just want you gone. You sign these forms here, here and here and I get you washed and on a plane, passport or no passport, back to England where you can get more fucked up in your own back yard. Capiche?"

Capiche. I signed. I was gone.

Chapter Twenty Three: Out of the Frying Pan Straight into Another One

At Heathrow there was a lot of fuss and a lot of questions. I gave a false address so my parents wouldn't be bothered. In those balmy days not everyone was a terrorist and only the chosen few were paranoid, so the Immigration Officers let it run for a few hours, then dismissed me as a lunatic who was so head-fucked I would be incapable of putting on my socks, let alone be a danger to anyone, and let me go. One of them even gave me five bob to get home. I went straight to Annie's. I knew once we were together everything would be fine. I had forgotten she never wanted to see me again. Her mother opened the door and looked at me as if I was a dog turd.

"You look terrible. What on earth have you been doing?"

I resisted the urge to tell the truth, whatever that was. "I've been on a religious retreat to purify my mind and body so that I would be worthy of your daughter's love," I said.

"What a lying degenerate you are," she said.

"I'll pray for you, Mrs. Beauchamp. Can I see Annie?"

"No, and anyway she's engaged to a nice young man from the co-op." She closed the door. I'd been told that when one door closes another opens, but like most things I'd been told it was complete bollocks. I couldn't remember when I'd last eaten and knew I'd lost weight because my jeans kept slipping dangerously low. I caught sight of myself in a shop window and almost jumped back in alarm. A cadaverous, hollow-eyed maniac stared back at me. I looked jumpy and deranged, a clockwork monkey on speed, an animated coat hanger. How had all this happened? I was only nineteen. At least I had the comforting memory of my Moroccan revolution. The only things that could spoil that memory were the facts. I wandered all night and at four in the morning found myself near St. Paul's Cathedral. I wished John Donne was still Dean there. I could go in and tell him how much I love his writing, especially the love poetry before he discovered God:

And now good morrow to our waking souls,

Which watch not one another out of fear;
For love, all love of other sights controls,
And makes one little room, an everywhere.

I was over three hundred years too late. I thought it would be nice to have friends from different ages. Everyone would choose famous people, of course, but I'd choose the forgotten of history: the bloke who cleared up all the elephant poo for Hannibal, the first caveman to draw a picture on a wall, Babylonian ladies of the night for the stories they could tell, a medieval executioner, one of the last banshees before the Romans slaughtered them all. I lay down in the little churchyard and fell asleep with the line in my head: "One short sleep past will wake eternally/And death shall be no more; Death thou shalt die." When I awoke I was cold and shivering. I thought John Donne was sitting next to me, though I couldn't see him. The line "Be thine own palace, or the world's thy jail" snapped into my mind. Is that what we'd all been doing in the past few years with our celebration of self and world changing ideas, trying to be our own brightly painted palaces before the world nails you to the road? I got up and wandered around. I stopped at a sign: The Samaritans. I'd had it with God but the Samaritan was probably just an ordinary bloke trying to help out a poor sod who'd been mugged. I went in, down some narrow steps and into an office. A pale Jewish girl looked up from a battered typewriter. I thought of asking her to marry me. She looked sad and sensible.

"Hello. Can I help?" She asked.

"What do you have in mind?" I said.

"We could talk."

"If you'd like to. I'll listen."

She smiled. "No, I could listen and you could talk. Is something wrong?"

"With what?"

"I'll make some coffee."

I don't know what I said, but it was obviously strange brew because an hour later she was dragging me across London to the Maudsley Psychiatric Hospital. The moment I met Dr. Lewis I knew we were destined not to understand each other and to become enemies for ever and ever amen. He looked like a Nazi dentist behind his glittering spectacles. We spoke in what I thought was a desultory manner for about half an hour: I told him about God being a vicious maniac who didn't exist anyway; about Parks and Recreation being a home for the psychotic and mentally ill and which suited me fine until I went to university to become a clever bastard; about the global conspiracy to turn us all into morons and how the polar bear in Central Park was the only fucker in New York to understand that the agents of destruction were going to steal our power to make our own reality and create a riparian paradise; and how the crowning jewel in my short life had been the revolution I'd masterminded in Morocco. I was all talked out and got up to go. In a twinkle the good doctor was out of his chair and barring the door. He said, with a smile like a damp tea towel, that he thought I was very ill but that he could help and that he had the power to section me for thirty days. It was an arrest by the thought police and I'd fallen straight into it. Was there no end to my stupidity?

Chapter Twenty Four: Out of Our Heads in Bedlam

I was taken to Bethlem Royal Hospital in Kent. What they don't tell you about mental hospitals is that the psychiatrists are more fucked up than the patients, and more dangerous because they think they are sane. The fundamental difference between the sane and the insane, as Hunter Thompson was to observe, is that the sane have the power to lock up the insane and not vice versa. Yes, some of the people in psychiatric hospitals are miserable, depressed, delusional, pathetic, unable to distinguish reality from their own mad dreams, hopeless at everyday life, but those are just the staff, and it could as easily be a description of parliament.

Doctors give people drugs that turn them from ordinarily unhappy people into complete mental cases. This then justifies the existence of mental hospitals, and, of course, their high salaried jobs. The less time I spent wittering away my thoughts on religion, the more I seemed to understand how power worked in the world, and it was terrifying. My first day there was the best. There was a fight at breakfast, which was interesting to watch until the cutlery started flying, then I spent an hour listening to a nobhead called Derek who told me that the brain is like a jar of energy, and the lid has to be unscrewed occasionally to let out the steam, but that he had forgotten how to perform this cathartic technique, so every now and then he went apeshit and tried to throw people off tall buildings. He said the only reason he hadn't succeeded was that he had acute acrophobia and hated heights so much that he was violently sick if he even lifted one leg, which made walking a problem. He shuffled with his feet on the ground and never looked up. I shared a dorm with two others – Robert, a medical student who was suffering from compulsive disorder behaviour; he was obsessed with dirt and would wash his clothes and body constantly. His treatment was that every morning a nurse would smear him all over with mud and he had to leave it on. Welcome to the sophisticated twentieth century. I liked Robert; he laughed at his own neuroses and could play blues piano. The other dorm mate was a boxer called Charlie who'd completely fallen apart. He stayed in bed and wept. When I met his wife I could see why he'd had a breakdown. She had the sting of a wasp and treated him like a lip sore. She had taught their son to spit in Charlie's face. It was she who should be locked up.

In the afternoon I was assessed. Dr. Lewis did a boring word association test – why do they always say 'mother'? – and then asked me if I took drugs. I said it was very kind of him to offer but I'd given them up, and he should think of doing so too. He said he thought I had considerable difficulty in distinguishing between what was real and what wasn't, and sometimes I made up things. I said I thought I might have made him up and I was sorry for making such a mess of it. He didn't laugh but made a note in his big black n'red book. He asked if I was aware that some of the things I said were, in effect, lies. I said they weren't, in effect, lies, they were, in effect, truths I'd made up. He made another note. He said I exhibited extreme symptoms of paranoia. I said that surely he must know that a paranoiac is just a person in full possession of the facts. Finally he said he thought I was schizophrenic. I said that wasn't a very nice thing to say to either of us. If I'd known the consequences of this conversation, I would have handled it differently. I should have realised that joking to a man with the eyes of a nazi dentist who has had a humour bypass operation is a dangerous occupation. I had two more days of freedom.

I talked to lost souls. Many of them were just sadly human. Jo, the biker girl who had been in a crushing motorcycle accident and watched the two halves of her boyfriend carried solemnly to an ambulance, and now wanted to join him on the highway somewhere else. Chain smoking Jenny, her soul naked as a burnt twig, frail as icicles, who, perhaps like most of the human race, found life a mine field and just to get through the day without losing a major piece of herself was a triumph. Graham, a man with terrified cerulean eyes who laughed inappropriately and looked in constant pain, as if he had been nailed to a glacier. And these were the nurses. The patients were slightly more sane. James, a failed actor whose life was a harvest of stones and who would suddenly sit on the ground, head in hands, as the weight of everything descended on him. David, constitutionally earnest and just plain odd, who told me that what he really wanted in life was to undress with a girl, then masturbate but stop before the crucial moment, and then get dressed and take her to a Wimpy bar. Ted, a failed writer who had convinced himself he was a Vietnam war vet who had a bullet lodged in his brain that gave him demonic dreams, despite the fact he was Welsh and the furthest he'd travelled was Belgium. He looked like a chubby fourteen year old boy constantly on the verge of tears. He hated Derek to the extent that he told me he had an elaborate plan to murder him and make it look like suicide. Daisy, a fifty year old woman who had no idea where she was and who wore a little girl's frock and plimsolls and skipped up and down the corridors. Sue, a lost kind soul who would never make it to thirty. Jane, a romantic failed suicide. All these seemed like ordinary human beings to me.

A Japanese male nurse called Jay asked me why I was in the hospital. I told him I was the resurrected Che Guevara who had started a revolution in Morocco and New York, and was now going to make England a Republic. A sun lit up in his head and he beamed. He said this was just what he needed for his dissertation – a humdinger lunatic who identified with a historical figure to the extent that they no longer knew who they were. He followed me around for the next three hours asking questions and taking notes. I told him how, once Castro and I had liberated Cuba, I got bored with women and rum and fat cigars and craved the adrenalin rush of fighting reactionary forces in jungles against the odds and risking a romantic death in the arms of a flaxen haired beauty with a belt of bullets across her majestic breasts. How in Havana I lay in a bath with golden taps shaped like mermaids, but dreamed of hillsides and long nights in a blanket under the cold stars, smoking and drinking cheap brandy with my revolutionary comrades. About my final, fatal trip to Bolivia, when the dirty American army dragged me from a hut, emaciated and sick, arms out like Christ, and beat me to death. Jay said he'd get an A plus for his dissertation.

Then I ran out of things to say about Che and told him I'd had an apocalyptic revelation and, in fact, I wasn't Che Guevara, but Guy Fawkes. Jay's eyes misted, his face crumpled, he looked at his notebook and saw his A plus disappearing. I thought he was going to cry. I told him life was full of contradictions and he should embrace them and now he could write about Guy Fawkes, but the heart had gone out of it and he became quite depressed thereafter.

Chapter Twenty Five: Tragic Love and Moronic Happiness

Dr Lewis introduced a joint mentoring programme in which loonies were paired up and spent an hour or so each day trying to help each other, listening and talking. I was paired with Jane, a suicidal manic depressive who had tried to kill herself three times because of failed love affairs. He said he thought we shared a strange sensitivity that might be mutually beneficial. We sat in the day room with cups of brackish tea, watching David play the piano with the lid down.

"Maybe if I have cosmetic surgery men will love me. I could have my boobs made bigger, my chin flattened out," Jane said. It sounded a bit boring. "What would you have done?" she asked.

"I'd have a nipple put on my forehead and every time I fondled it an interesting idea would be stimulated, or a strong thought. I'd have one giant ear, so I could hear a mouse breathe a mile away. And I'd have extra knees put on the back of my legs so they'd bend both ways. Think of the footballing skills you'd develop."

Jane was looking at me very strangely.

"I want to be in love and happy," she said.

"Why?"

"What do you mean – why? Everyone wants to be in love and happy. All my love affairs are tragic."

"But all love is tragic," I said. "It has to be because it always ends – all kinds of love, sexual, romantic, platonic, they all end, because someone leaves through death, boredom, betrayal, illness. It always ends in sadness and loss and being alone. All love is tragic."

She looked even more depressed, but I was on a roll.

"And anyway, what kind of love are we talking about? Destructive love, jealous love, god love that makes people throughout history go off armed to the eyeballs and slaughter countless others who love something different?"

Jane was nearly in tears. "But it isn't wrong to want to be happy. Doctor Lewis says if I keep taking the medication and stay in hospital until I'm better there's no reason why I shouldn't live a happy life."

"He would say that. His job depends on deluding people. But happiness is a myth. It's for the moronic and mentally ill."

"But I am mentally ill," she said.

"Exactly. That's my point. Happiness is a loony idea so only a loony would want to pursue it. Being happy is merely celebrating other people's misery, because if everyone was happy it would be a meaningless thing. Happiness is a bubble we experience temporarily, a momentary joy, a by product of something else, then it's gone because it has to go. The pursuit of happiness is a sure way to depression. And how do you measure it – give people a happiness test?"

Where was all this was coming from? I watched the words pour from me in stupefied horror. Did I believe any of it? I had no idea, but I couldn't stop. "Happiness is an illusion caused by the temporary absence of reality. Graham Greene said: "Point me out the happy man and I will point you out egotism, selfishness, evil - or else an absolute ignorance." It's like the hippy idea of a perfect society, everyone living in harmony and peace and free love. Utopia is a logical impossibility. Nature does not permit it. In utopia, there is no loss of life. No obstacles to overcome. Therefore no humanity. Therefore no humanly conceived utopia. Presumably in a utopia everyone is free, but that freedom is an irrelevancy because everything is perfect. And anyway – what kind of freedom? To murder, to steal, to have more than others, to eat animals? Your utopia starts to disintegrate the moment you examine it. Love isn't free, it comes at a price and it's tragic anyway, as I've explained. We have to accept that most of what we do in life will fail. Take you, you're even a failed suicide."

Jane was sobbing uncontrollably now and later that night tried to commit suicide again. A nurse asked me what I'd done to upset her, but I couldn't remember anything I'd said. The next day Doctor Lewis took me off the joint mentoring programme and told me he was putting me on medication. When he was out of the room I peeked at his notes and he'd put in big letters by my name: 'MAY NOT BE A DANGER TO SELF BUT

CERTAINLY IS TO OTHERS.' Great. I picked up a biro and scribbled BOLLOCKS through his note. This wasn't a wise or grown up thing to do, but any mental patient could have told him 'mentoring pairs' was a crap idea. The blind leading the blind. Lots of people were in there because of drug abuse and were now being abused with drugs. It didn't make any sense. Increasingly, nothing made any sense. Perhaps that was what enlightenment is – realising that there is no meaning, no enlightenment, no heaven. We are all a little bit of self-torturing debris left over from the collision of matter and anti-matter.

Then I was summoned to the dorm and, without even the dignity of a private room, with Robert watching as he itched to scrape the mud off his clothes, suicidal Jo gave me my first injection of largactil. A big horsey dose right up the arse. Three hours later I knew what it was to be mentally ill.

Chapter Twenty Six: Lunacy and Walking Around the Ping Pong Table

Largactil reduces you. Your sense of self shrinks to a terror of how to get through the next minute and how long you can leave it before smoking the next cigarette. You are dull and paranoid. Everything seems too much effort, even your acute panic is exhausted. You cannot read because you cannot concentrate and thought is a distant country. Then the physical effects kick in: you cannot keep still although you feel constantly exhausted; you walk and walk and walk, even in circles. Your arms rise in an absurd parody of a sleepwalker's pose. Your mouth dries to dust and your lips crack. You sometimes get lockjaw and cannot eat or drink. Your brain is a poor terrified creature chained to a wheel as you wander round and round and round. Anyone watching would think you are a prize winning fruitcake, which is partly the point of the thing. You become a timid junkie, begging for the stelizene which will partly, temporarily, offset the effects of the largactil. Doctor Lewis often used this as a control – sometimes you got it, sometimes you didn't. His argument was that your behaviour was a manifestation of serious mental illness, not the effects of the drug. The fact you have never behaved like this before wasn't addressed. The power shifts entirely to the psychiatrist and your incapacitated self will admit you have been ill for years because you cannot summon up enough rationality to disagree coherently, and because you are too distressed to bother. Forever after, the sound of fear for me was the metallic tap of a hypodermic needle on a metal bowl.

After two weeks I was a zombie. I was given modicate and largactil, in varying doses. Dr. Lewis told my parents he thought I'd been seriously mentally ill for years and would never be able to live an ordinary life, perhaps not even hold down a simple job. Gilly came to see me and told me I was a stupid bastard and they'd got me now, which was true on both counts. A young psychiatrist tried to seduce her in the lift and she told him to shove his collected Freud up his ugly arse.

I spent many hours with my arms outstretched following David round and round the ping pong table, until we were both beyond exhaustion. If they'd wired us up we could have generated enough electricity to run the hospital. When I wasn't walking I was rocking in a chair, hugging myself. Sometimes I shuffled down to the compound where they kept baboons used for experimentation in the hospital. This was a rhesus concentration camp. I liked the baboons, their frightened animated energy and quick intelligent eyes were so much livelier than the vegetable I'd become. A month before I would have liberated and armed them, with instructions to shoot on sight, but now I could only stare moronically at them. They knew this was a death factory, and that what lay ahead was pain and terror. I'd seen that look on the chimps they sent up in space. The scientists tried to kid us it was joy and laughter, but that rictus grin as they were strapped in the capsule was cold terror.

Psychiatric drugs strip you of choice. You cannot even summon the will to say No. The drugs I had chosen to take when I was free were a strange brew. Mostly, they sent my brain on an unspecified pilgrimage to uncharted territories. Some landscapes were best left unvisited, some were gory and battle-worn, some had a whiff of heaven in the jasmine and nectar that brewed and blossomed there, some let the senses off the leash of the self and scampered and played on their own, bringing back fresh stores of things tasted, touched and felt. Then you returned, carrying a bloody angel's wing fresh from battle or a flower some forgotten nymph gave you. Whereas they took you somewhere, psychiatric drugs only took you prisoner. There is the madness of liberation, and the madness of control. "Madness is silenced by reason," said Foucault, and I had become quietly mummified. I spent hours looking at the self portraits of a nineteenth century patient hanging in a little museum in the hospital. In the first he looked a bit wild, but excited about life, how I imagine a young William Blake. Nine portraits later he had disintegrated to a mad aged wreck with only a broken light in the eyes to show there was still a human being trapped in that pitiful frame.

In the mornings I was taken to Occupational Therapy, where a Belgian woman who looked like Elsie Tanner taught me how to use a sewing machine. I made myself a big, baggy, striped prisoner's suit and wore it day and night, much to Dr. Lewis's annoyance. Mental patients also make profitable industrial slaves. Many spent mornings putting cutlery in boxes for a local industry. Letting the suicidal roam in a landscape of sharp metal objects had a beautiful, moronic irony. Who got paid for this? Not the patients. Dr. Lewis now appeared to me as a walking sneer. I wished I could sleep away the rest of my life but sleep was often a forbidden country and when it came proved to be a dangerous bedfellow, with dull contaminated dreams of freedom that laughed at me. The angel at my shoulder had become prince of goblins.

One evening I was pacing up and down outside the bathroom. A sailor called Andrew had been in there for five hours. He could never move on to the next activity, twitched constantly, and had memorised the singles charts, A and B sides, from May 1965 to June 1970. His treatment, for bizarre reasons no one could understand, least of all him, was to tie his arms to his side, put a rubber ring around him and throw him in the swimming pool. I had thought life was a strange adventure that I wanted to embrace as fully as I could. Now I thought that by and large I'd be better off dead. I sat on the floor rocking gently, hugging my knees.

"Oh my God." I looked up. It was April, my old Religious Studies Teacher of the glorious and joyful sex in the tent. That now seemed a lifetime ago. She heard what had befallen me and drove down from Leeds. She had spoken to Dr. Lewis and been granted permission to take me out for half an hour, no more. She was to stay with me at all times and not, under any circumstances, allow me to drink alcohol, which he said would combine with the drugs and possibly bring on a complete psychotic breakdown. With that in mind she took me straight to the nearest pub and bought me a pint of Guinness and a whisky chaser. It was a balmy evening. I said my only friends were baboons. She said that didn't surprise her. She said Dr. Lewis told her that if I showed any signs of odd behaviour she was to take me straight back to the hospital, and that's when she knew he was mad, because my behaviour had always been odd. That was normal. What was scary was this timid indolence.

She said she had a plan. It was very simple. She would drive me somewhere and we would have abundant sex for a few days, and drink lots of wine, then I'd be alright, and she would go back to Leeds, where she taught Religious Studies in a big comprehensive school. This sounded like an excellent plan. Roxy Music's *Virginia Plain* was playing very loudly and this seemed to confirm the excellence, though I wasn't sure why. We stocked up on cigarettes and I had another pint of Guinness. I told her that the drugs made me impotent, and she said "The drugs haven't met me yet." Two hectic, blissful days later, in a borrowed flat, after huge amounts of wine and gleeful sex I started to feel human again. The largactil was still there, like a shadow I'd swallowed that was waiting to swallow me, but in the glory of our hedonism it definitely seemed to be waning. She went back to Leeds. I went to my parents and told them that they should ignore all calls from Dr. Lewis, who it turned out, I told them, was a child molesting, dog abusing, Nazi sympathizer. This did it for my dear Mum, who loved dogs. And so it transpired that my angel wasn't a feathery winged bloke at my shoulder, but a nymphomaniac Religious Studies teacher from Leeds.

I had escaped the Thought Police and the agents of control who knew that the dangerous doomed dreams of the 60s and early 70's could change the world, so had set about systematically crushing them, but how long could I elude these forces of iniquity? I had foolishly told policemen and psychiatrists and everyone really about the dark plot to contain us all and how only the enlightenment of revolution could stop it. On reflection, it may have been wiser to keep my mouth shut, but it was done and I would simply have to tread carefully and keep a vigilant watch on events. I needed a safe haven for a few months.

I was just about to telephone to get my old job back at Parks and Recreation when I got a call from Peter's parents. Come quickly, his Dad said, his tears salting the telephone line.

Chapter Twenty Seven: One Drops Back in the Cuckoo's Nest

The police had picked up Peter several times and brought him home. He'd gone AWOL again. We drove around for an hour or so, chain smoking, in his dad's battered Cortina. His thin hair was slicked back with brylcreem, enhancing big flappy ears. His skin was rubbery and grey. He looked like a sick wing nut. The largactil was still making threats inside my head but they seemed to be further away now, like children backing off to a safe distance before throwing stones and hurling insults. I suggested we stop the car and walk around. This was mostly because Peter's dad was singing Jim Reeves *Distant Drums* over and over in a miserable nicotined baritone. I couldn't stand it. I hated Jim Reeves songs and when he died in a plane crash I couldn't help thinking he'd been singing *Distant Drums* and the pilot finally had enough and headed straight for a mountain. Also, the car was so full of smoke we couldn't see anyway.

We parked and agreed to cover the Edmonton Green area, then meet up in half an hour by the Town Hall. The glorious days of the market and pearly Kings and Queens and old black and white timbered shops had gone and been replaced by an ugly precinct. When I finally got my revolution going the Beatles *White Album*, The Stones *Beggars Banquet* and Hendrix's *Bold as Love* would be played very loudly as machinery destroyed the precinct and returned it to its former living warmth and smell of vegetables and fruit. I'd had many happy days there as a child, stealing and bantering and delivering groceries on a bike and waiting until I was old enough to smoke and kiss girls and get into serious trouble.

Outside a glass fronted cheap lingerie shop about a dozen people were in a semi circle. A few were staring. A few were sneering. I knew before I saw him that this was Peter. He was sitting crosslegged on a sack. He was wearing another sack. His hair and eyebrows were shaved off. He hadn't washed for a week or so to judge by the smell. I bent down to him.

"Peter. It's me. Look at me." But he wouldn't. Whether by ill fate or choice, and I suspected both, he would not meet my eyes. He had placed himself in another country. I didn't mind that, I'd done it myself often enough, but it all seemed so damned miserable. Madness should run free, not end up like a chilled and unwashed John the fucking Baptist in the backside of a London suburb. I got angry and shook his shoulders and lifted him up. He suddenly looked at me with such venom I thought he was going to headbutt me into next week.

"The Lord said: I came to bring a sword!" He shouted in my face in a stink of halitosis.

"That doesn't mean you can't brush your fucking teeth!" I shouted back, though I was scared. I turned on the small crowd. "Just go away, all of you. Go on. Fuck off! This is a private conversation."

Everyone stayed put.

"Peter, there is no god. Once you grasp that, you're free," I said.

He stared at me fiercely, as if I were all the enemies he'd ever had.

"So it's made you free, has it?" He shouted.

"Well, I did nearly get killed by a camel, and by gangs in New York, and then I got locked up in a loony bin by the forces of darkness, but I was speaking metaphorically."

"I've renounced the world," he said.

"But the world won't renounce you. It'll fuck you up. There are dark forces that don't want anything to change."

"Satan, get thee behind me."

"Yes, but also the bastards in suits who run everything. And anyway, you don't want Satan behind you, that way he can stick a pitchfork up your arse. You want him in front of you where you can look him in the eye and take the fucker on."

I looked behind and Peter's dad was standing there with big tears on his rubbery cheeks. He looked like a wizened little boy who needed a cuddle. I wished I hadn't mentioned the loony bin, because that's exactly where Peter was taken a few hours later.

Now I had a problem. I promised Peter's dad I would visit him within a few days, but he was also in Bethlem and the staff would recognise me. Dr. Lewis would get his needles back into me and pretty soon I'd be following David around the ping pong table again. A few days later I borrowed a dark suit, tied up my hair under a trilby and wore huge dark glasses. No one would know me. I was safe. I walked down the corridor.

"Hi Steve," said David.

"Steve's back!" shouted Daisy.

"Shut the fuck up, you lunatics!" I ran down the corridor and into the dorm. Peter was sitting on the bed, rocking gently. Shit. They'd started already. His lips were almost white. Something had broken in him.

"Hello Steve. I love you. I have so many friends here. And last night, the man opposite spoke in his sleep. He said "Don't forget the gate." And I heard a gate creaking as it closed."

"That's great, Peter. You have the gift. But you've got to get out of here. We could find two delightful women of relaxed virtue. We could take our drugs of choice. We could go to the Buddhist Temple. We could start a band. You can join my revolution."

He'd stopped listening and was looking out of the window at something only he could see. He'd gone. He reminded me of myself a short time ago.

When I got home a letter was waiting. I'd got a place at University. I was going to be a clever bastard. I'd find revolutionary comrades and sparkling intellects to inspire the new world we'd build. I'd find poets and idealists and thinkers. People would hunch in dark corners, chain smoking and reading Jean Paul Sartre. Quantum physics would be discussed late into the night. Brilliant theologians would posit entirely gratuitous new versions of God. I went to see Peter a few more times, then left London. I was hungry for everything again.

Chapter Twenty Eight: Everything Bleeds Eventually

It took me approximately twenty four hours to discover that universities weren't temples for clever bastards. They were full of young people determined to drink away the best three years of their lives, get laid often and do as little work as was humanly possible. Conversations were mostly about hangovers and how few lectures they attended. Academics seemed to be stupid with self entrancement. There were exceptions, but there are always exceptions. However, there was music, and theatre, and time to read. I decided that for a while I would try not to bring great disasters upon myself.

I got a letter from Peter in big infantile letters. "Dear Steve, How are you, my sister is well, I am well I hope you are well. Please come and see me. Love Peter." I decided to wait until half term. Peter couldn't wait. The world doesn't turn according to our own caprice. I got a short letter from his mum. He was dead. He'd been found floating in the canal. The funeral was the following week. It didn't make sense. Peter was terrified of water.

I went straight down to London. Somehow he got out of hospital and went to St. Albans Church. Why? No one knows. His parents are all grief and confusion. The priest took a liking to his prophetic ramblings and gave him an attic room in the church buildings. It was difficult not to like Peter. He was both powerful and helpless. I ask and no one knows what happened the night he died. Now it's a murder story: who killed Peter? The major suspects: me; his parents; his culture; god; himself; a psychiatrist; the heavenly longings of a lost generation that now seem silly and heartbreaking. I have to go back to go forward. It's dark, troubled, misty, a night of shadows and possibilities. A night for disorder. He lay in the dark, his narrowed ocean-blue eyes staring at the ceiling. He clears his throat. I hear him. It's a building where sound carries. Then he almost hears a voice. He strains to catch it in the dark. He mutters a prayer. His lips are dry, parched. He wants to know what it is, this calling that is elusive and compelling, like a bird or a star.

He gets up and dresses swiftly – worn denim jeans and a denim shirt. He is thin, pale, and haunted. His cheekbones are prominent and make him look almost oriental. It is cold but he doesn't shiver as he follows the church path between the grey graves like great rotting teeth sticking up from the earth. Then the lane in semi darkness, the few houses either side long ago tucked up, the field beyond. What is it? That thing, that something that masqueraded as a voice and is so beguiling? He has to find out. He must know. Is this what everything has been about? This dewy grass on a dark night? He keeps walking. He doesn't even notice the oily black water, thick in its own secret. Was this it? A trick or a mystery? Panic and the useless flapping and bubbling. It seems to take hours before things become warm again. Death is always a stranger approaching with a rusty nail or a voice almost calling from the dark night.

We wait on the corner of the two up two down street. A lot of people have come and neighbours stand at their gates. Peter's Dad next to me has shrunk considerably. The dead hasten the deaths of the living. He smokes another cigarette and then says, "Here he comes. Bless him." And a great glossy black funeral limo chugs into view. They always make me think of high class pimp's cars. On top is a monstrous guitar made out of blue flowers. It is a baroque, well intentioned, flashy gesture that makes me want to smile. I go in the family car, pinioned between the grieving shrunken father and the frozen mother who never made it any secret that she adored her son more than she ever did her husband. What is extraordinary is that more people don't go mad, considering that most of them are forced to live in families. At the cemetery, there are more people. Some blacks from the revivalist group, a Buddhist monk, a few Parks and Recreation people that I invited, a few druggies, some of the mental patients, ex-wife Gail. It is starting to have a carnival atmosphere, but with menace in the air.

The priest begins. He waffles for a few minutes and is clearly annoyed by the revivalists who shout "Halleluiah" and "Praise the Lord" after every cliché he utters. Then some of the mental patients join in by shouting obscenities to complement the alleluiahs.

"Peter is now with our Lord whom he worshipped so intensely."

"Hallelujah! Praise Jesus!"

"Fuck bugger arsewipe!"

Then the priest plays Bob Dylan's "Blowing in the Wind" because Peter loved Dylan, as we all do. It is a gesture towards contemporaneity. Something about it makes me sick. Back at the house it all gets heightened. The Revivalists are having a whoopee meeting in the little back yard, which incenses Peter's mum. "Bloody blacks shouting and hollering when I've only just buried my Pete," she says, even though Peter was cremated. I drink a lot of whisky. A fracas starts at the front gate. David the gentle mental patient has asked Gail if he can masturbate with her and then take her to a wimpy bar. He fondles one of her breasts and the Buddhist monk jumps on him and gets him in a half nelson. Mad Daisy is lifting her skirt and showing her arse to an octogenarian in a wheelchair. Charlie the little deranged boxer punches the lights out of a local herpes-ridden drug dealer, just for something to do, I suppose. The Priest calls for some decorum on a day such as this and I tell him to fuck off, because it feels good to tell a Priest to fuck off. One of the druggies puts acid in the beer barrel. Someone puts on the Faces singing "Stay With Me" and a few of Peter's old band mates start jiving in the street. Peter's ashes get knocked all over the jelly and trifle but the kids eat it anyway and share it with a fine little dog.

I look up at a cloud that looks like Peter. It's time for me to leave the party. Which is what I do.

THE END

Biography

Steve Attridge has had over 100 TV scripts produced. Twice a BAFTA nominee, he has also won 3 RTS Awards (for Best Drama), Best Film Award 2 Writer's Guild Awards and TV film awards. He has had 7 films produced.

He has 24 books published, including adult fiction, psychological thrillers, children's, history, comedy. This year his latest book was published by *WildWolf*, a dystopian futuristic story but with heart and characteristic gallows humour, called *Sometimes I Disappear*. His novel, *The Natural Law*, went straight to number one in the Amazon Kindle Singles Bestsellers. He won an Eric Gregory Award for Poetry and a slam poetry award. Nine of his stage plays have been produced and he has performed 2 one man shows at the Edinburgh Festival.

This year he is producing a series of children's books called The Urban Fox. He is also writing a historical novel and a biography of a reformed criminal. He has worked as a Writer and Lecturer all over the world, running Masterclasses, short courses and University Courses, including at Oxford, Warwick and Sheffield.

He ran writing workshops at the New York Public library and often runs Guardian Masterclass events.

For more information and regular writing tips go to steveattridge.com
https://www.facebook.com/profile.php?id=100092356581102

Printed in Great Britain
by Amazon

24206151R00086